Religions
of the World

Judaism

Laurel Corona

LUCENT
BOOKS®

THOMSON
★
™
GALE

San Diego • Detroit • New York • San Francisco • Cleveland • New Haven, Conn. • Waterville, Maine • London • Munich

To Rabbi Arthur Zuckerman and Rabbi David Kornberg.
Thank you for listening.

On cover: A Jewish man wearing a prayer shawl and yarmulke
reads from his prayer book in front of a Torah.

LIBRARY OF CONGRESS CATALOGING-IN-PUBLICATION DATA

Corona, Laurel, 1949–
    Judaism / by Laurel Corona.
       p. cm. — (Religions of the world)
    Summary: Discusses the historical origins, teachings, practices, persecution,
spread, and challenges of Judaism.
    Includes bibliographical references and index.
    ISBN 1-56006-987-2 (hc)
    1. Judaism—Juvenile literature. [1. Judaism.] I. Title II. Series: Religions of the
world (San Diego, Calif.)
    BM573.C68 2003
    296—dc21

2002013089

Contents

Foreword

Religion has always been a central component of human culture, though its form and practice have changed through time. Ancient people lived in a world they could not explain or comprehend. Their world consisted of an environment controlled by vague and mysterious powers attributed to a wide array of gods. Artifacts dating to a time before recorded history suggest that the religion of the distant past reflected this world, consisting mainly of rituals devised to influence events under the control of these gods.

The steady advancement of human societies brought about changes in religion as in all other things. Through time, religion came to be seen as a system of beliefs and practices that gave meaning to—or allowed acceptance of—anything that transcended the natural or the known. And, the belief in many gods ultimately was replaced in many cultures by the belief in a Supreme Being.

As in the distant past, however, religion still provides answers to timeless questions: How, why, and by whom was the universe created? What is the ultimate meaning of human life? Why is life inevitably followed by death? Does the human soul continue to exist after death, and if so, in what form? Why is there pain and suffering in the world, and why is there evil?

In addition, all the major world religions provide their followers with a concrete and clearly stated ethical code. They offer a set of moral instructions, defining virtue and evil and what is required to achieve goodness. One of these universal moral codes is compassion toward others above all else. Thus, Judaism, Christianity, Islam, Hinduism, Buddhism, Confucianism, and Taoism each teach a version of the so-called golden rule, or in the words of Jesus Christ, "As ye would that men should do to you, do ye also to them likewise." (Luke 6:31) For example, Confucius instructed his disciples to "never impose on others what you would not choose for yourself." (*Analects*: 12:2) The Hindu epic poem, Mahabharata, identifies the core of all Hindu teaching as not doing unto others what you do not wish done to yourself. Similarly Muhammad declared that no Muslim could be a true believer unless he desired for his brother no less than that which he desires for himself.

It is ironic, then, that although compassionate concern for others forms the heart of all the major religions' moral teachings, religion has also been at the root of countless conflicts throughout history. It has been suggested that much of the appeal that religions hold for humankind lies in their unswerving faith in the truth of their particular vision. Throughout history, most religions have shared a profound confidence that their interpretation of life, God, and the universe is the right one, thus giving their followers a sense of certainty in an uncertain and often fragile existence. Given the assurance displayed by most religions regarding the fundamental correctness of their teachings and practices, it is perhaps not surprising that religious intolerance has fueled disputes and even full-scale wars between peoples and nations time and time again, from the Crusades of medieval times to the current bloodshed in Northern Ireland and the Middle East.

Today, as violent religious conflicts trouble many parts of our world, it has become more important than ever to learn about the similarities as well as the differences between faiths. One of the most effective ways to accomplish this is by examining the beliefs, customs, and values of various religions. In the Religions of the World series, students will find a clear description of the core creeds, rituals, ethical teachings, and sacred texts of the world's major religions. In-depth explorations of how these faiths changed over time, how they have influenced the social customs, laws, and education of the countries in which they are practiced, and the particular challenges each one faces in coming years are also featured.

Extensive quotations from primary source materials, especially the core scriptures of each faith, and a generous number of secondary source quotations from the works of respected modern scholars are included in each volume in the series. It is hoped that by gaining insight into the faiths of other peoples and nations, students will not only gain a deeper appreciation and respect for different religious beliefs and practices, but will also gain new perspectives on and understanding of their own religious traditions.

One God, One People, Many Voices

"Hear O Israel, the Lord is our God, the Lord Is One." These words at the beginning of the Hebrew prayer known as the Shema lie at the heart of Judaism. Other people may worship other gods, but to the Jews only the Lord, known in Hebrew as Adonai, is God. The Shema goes on to say that Adonai is to be revered and worshiped with everything humans possess—their hearts, souls, and all other resources. He is to be thought of and talked about when going to bed and when rising, when walking in the street and in the home—in other words all day long, every day of one's life. Those who love Adonai in this manner will find their lives blessed.

This is the essence of Judaism. The history of the Jewish people, as told in the Hebrew Bible (known to Christians as the Old Testament and to Jews as the Tanakh) is the story of their attempts, mostly unsuccessful, to live up to the high standards of the deceptively simple statements of the Shema. What it really means to show love of God in one's actions has been the focal point of Jewish philosophical debate for several millenia, the heart of the rituals of Judaism today, and the source of some of its deepest conflicts.

Who Is a Jew?

Though the premise at the heart of the Shema is a simple and unifying one, very little else about Judaism is so uncomplicated. In fact, to many Jews today, Judaism as a faith and being Jewish as a person are barely related at all. Some have rejected the faith while remaining fiercely proud of the culture. Some go even further, claiming that being Jewish has little more meaning to their sense of identity than their height or hair color. For others, however, practice of the faith is the chief organizing principle of each day and the central factor in their identity. Jews differ widely in their views, therefore, but most would agree with Rabbi Stephen M. Wylen: "Culture, customs, ethics, sense of self—these are all part of Judaism as much as the faith and the rituals of the Jewish religion."[1]

However, some would take issue with Wylen. For some Judaism is a faith above all else. Within Judaism today there is a passionate controversy between the Orthodox and many other Jews. To the Orthodox, there is only one true form of Judaism, strict observance of all the commandments laid down in the Torah. Some Orthodox go so far as to say that Reform and Conservative Jews should be lumped in the same category as Christians or Muslims rather than as practicers of Judaism at all. Other disagreements about Jewish identity also divide Jews. Even the time-honored tradition of limiting the definition of Jew to those born of a Jewish mother has been eroded in recent years by Reform Judaism's inclusion of the offspring of Jewish fathers and non-Jewish mothers in situations where the child has been raised as a Jew. Orthodox Jews still feel that a formal conversion is required before these offspring can be regarded as Jews.

The Foundation of a Faith

Faith and identity are very different aspects of Judaism that have intertwined to a greater or lesser degree throughout its history. Still, it is possible to identify several components that unite Jews around the world. The first is acknowledgment that there is only one God; the second is reliance on the Torah as the source of moral law; the third is Hebrew as the unifying language of Jewish worship; the fourth is the land of Israel, which Jews feel was given to them by God; and the fifth is a deeply rooted sense that in spite of their diversity they are one people. The essence of Judaism as both a faith and an identity can be discerned by tracing its historical roots.

The Jews are the descendants of Abraham, probably (although not certainly) a real person who lived approximately four millenia ago. He established the first known community that was not based on where one came from or who one's family was. His community was based on faith. Abraham is credited with having introduced to the world the concept of "ethical monotheism," the belief in a single all-powerful God who is also the source of morality. Abraham's God laid down rules of ethics by which people were to live, then rewarded or punished them based on how they chose to act.

These rules were further clarified in the time of Moses, around 1200 B.C., by the revelation at Mount Sinai of the Ten Commandments and other sacred laws known as mitzvot. The Hebrews thus became the "people of the covenant," tied to God by an eternal contract whereby He agreed to protect and support them, including the promise of a homeland in the area of today's Israel, if they acted in accordance with His laws. The generally misunderstood term "chosen people" refers to this covenant. The Jews accepted Adonai as God and agreed to live by a higher and stricter moral code than those around them, and thus ensure their survival and prosperity as a people. In fact one traditional Jewish midrash (an explanatory story not found in the Bible) says that bigger and more powerful nations turned down God's offer of a covenant because it meant they would have to stop doing whatever they pleased, and that only the small tribe of Israelites was willing to take on the burden. Thus, they were "chosen."

The compilers and editors of the Bible, working many years after most of the events described therein, were not interested in providing merely an accurate historical record of how the Hebrew people came to follow a certain set of laws. They were tracing the evolution of a faith and the growth of its practitioners' identity as a single people. In this telling of history, God is the main character. Throughout the Bible, harm comes to the Israelites when they do not live up to the covenant, and reward comes when they do. By the end of the historical period covered by the

Moses displays the tablets containing the Ten Commandments to his followers. This event is part of a Jewish religious history that has spanned thousands of years.

Hebrew Bible, approximately 500 B.C., the religious foundation of Judaism around the importance of abiding by the covenant was complete. The rest, as a famous rabbi would say centuries later, is commentary.

Crisis and Continuity

Judaism, at its simplest, is therefore a monotheistic faith based on ethical principles and rituals de-signed to encourage not necessar-ily the easiest, but the highest pos-sible quality of life for its followers. History, however, is full of exam-ples of situations where being Jew-ish has caused great hardship. The most obvious example is the Holo-caust, where over 6 million died simply for being Jews. The Holo-caust was far from an isolated oc-currence, however. In the Middle Ages, Jews were blamed for such things as plagues, crop failure, and infant death. Jews tended to live in isolation from others, sometimes because they were forced to, but often by choice because their dietary laws, prohibitions on intermarriage, Saturday Sabbath, and other distinctions made interaction with non-Jews difficult. This made them easy targets in superstitious and ignorant societies manipulated by the two most powerful forces of the time: the Church and the monarchy.

Isolation had its costs, including making Jews easy targets for murderous anti-Semitic attacks, but it had its advantages as well, including the chance for a distinct Jewish identity and culture to evolve. It was only with mass immigration to western Europe, the United States, and elsewhere that the majority of Jews began to live outside of small, isolated, totally Jewish communities. The end of isolation had its costs too, as this insular Jewish way of life faded with immigrants' assimilation into the more diverse world of cities such as New York and Paris. Still, much of Jewish culture managed to survive and even thrive, including its cuisine, music, and religious festivals. Today there is scarcely any element of modern life that has not

been influenced by the culture and achievements of the Jews.

Judaism and the Jews Today

In the aftermath of World War II, Jewish culture was weakened by the devastating loss not only of those who died, but the future generations who were never born because the 1.5 million children who perished never reached parenthood. Today, some feel the future of Judaism is further weakened by the fact that Holocaust survivors are growing old, and before long the world will lose the last living witnesses of its horrors. Anne Frank, whose diary made her one of the most famous victims, would be in her mid-seventies if she had survived.

Yet, though few would attempt to argue that the Holocaust had any bright side, the Jews who survived did transform Judaism. Though many were broken in spirit and health, the energy of younger survivors, passionate about their identity as Jews, was vital to the creation of the State of Israel and the development of worldwide Jewish solidarity. Their children and grandchildren have inherited a faith revitalized in recent years by new movements as well. Today Jews have a range of options from

Anne Frank's diary exposed the evils of the Holocaust.

in these two places may feel some strength in numbers, but the smallness and vulnerability of the Jewish population worldwide can also be discerned from the same statistics. There are only approximately 13 million Jews in the world, and 80 percent live in the United States or Israel. This means that the experience of being Jewish remains an isolating one in the rest of the world. Taking Israel and the United States out of the equation, there are only approximately 2.5 million Jews scattered over the rest of the globe—the equivalent of the population of one large city. Traditional Jewish enclaves such as Russia and Ukraine today have Jewish populations of less than 0.5 percent. The thinness of the worldwide Jewish population is a matter of great concern because the growth of Islam (now more than a quarter of the world's population) and the anti-Israel sentiments of much of the world make small Jewish populations as vulnerable as ever to anti-Semitic attacks.

In the end, however, as much as Jews worry, most remain optimistic. Perhaps this optimism is the greatest legacy of their covenant

traditional Orthodox to New Age fusions of Jewish philosophy with Eastern meditative approaches. This has created more opportunities for Jews to find their way back to the faith.

But the future of Judaism is not an altogether rosy one. Approximately 45 percent of the world's Jews (around 6 million) live in the United States, and of this number approximately a third live in the New York area. Approximately 35 percent (around 4.5 million) live in Israel. Nine of the ten cities with the highest Jewish populations are in the United States or Israel. Jews

with God. Jews belong to something that had its beginnings with a thought about God in the desert. From this a people came to define themselves in terms of their relationship with that God. Judaism proclaims that that relationship is a joyous one. The Psalms exhort the Jews to shout and sing of the greatness of God and His creation.

"What is man that You are mindful of him?" Psalm 8 asks, to which there is no answer except gratitude and praise: "O Lord, our Lord, how majestic is Your name throughout the earth!"[2] Jews embrace whatever life holds, because to them all human beings are the children of God, but only they are the children of the covenant.

chapter | one

Patriarchs and Promises

Judaism is an ancient faith. It traces its roots back to the oldest known civilization in the world, Sumer, in the region known as Mesopotamia (today part of Turkey and Iraq), between the Tigris and Euphrates Rivers. What little is known about Mesopotamian civilization is largely a result of bits and pieces of writing etched into pottery or stone found in the rubble of ancient cities dating back

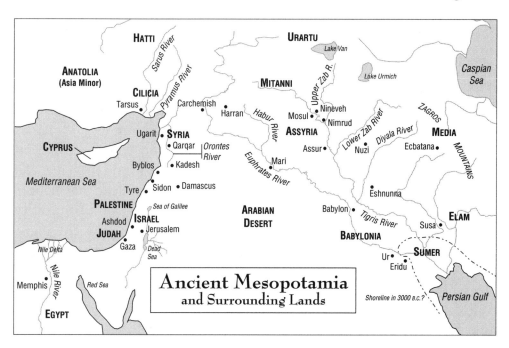

Ancient Mesopotamia
and Surrounding Lands

as far as 4000 B.C. Writing was invented in Sumer, and the first historical records, simple lists of names of kings, were developed there around 2500 B.C. It was in the Sumerian city of Ur, today considered to be the first city ever to develop on Earth, that Abraham was born sometime around 2000 B.C.

Because Abraham was not a king, no Sumerian record of him exists. Yet this man would create a legacy more profound and lasting than any of those whose names have been uncovered by archaeologists in the hot and dusty ruins of Mesopotamia's ancient cities. The reason for Abraham's stature in history is that he is credited with a momentous achievement: setting in motion a fundamental and lasting shift in religious belief that would lead over many centuries to the development of Judaism and, eventually, to Christianity and Islam as well.

Mesopotamians believed in many gods, having no better way to explain the awesome forces of nature and the regular cycles of the year. Each city had its own god, and people also chose individual gods; but despite great efforts to please these deities, misfortunes continued. They attributed floods, crop failures, illnesses, and such things to the gods' moods and whims, and they do not seem to have looked to their gods for guidance in resolving moral dilemmas in their personal or community life.

The God of Abraham

Abraham, according to the Bible, had a vision that he was to take his family and "set out on a journey for a destination that would be made known to him" later, and that as a result of undertaking this journey on faith alone, he would "father a great nation."[3] This vision came from a deity Abraham came to believe was the one true God, Adonai. Though Adonai demanded altars and sacrifices, as did other gods, mere adherence to ritual was not enough. People also had to avoid robbery, murder, adultery, and other forms of harm. Though there already were codes of law in Sumer by this point, they simply outlined what the punishments for crimes would be rather than focusing on how people should behave. To Abraham it was clear that people should follow a code of morality simply because it was the right thing to do, and that such righteousness was at the core of Adonai's will for His creation. Faith, therefore, could not be separated from good behavior.

One God, Many Names

Although the Bible says that Abraham "invoked the Lord by name," what name he used is not clear. In fact, there are many names by which God was known in biblical times. These include names derived from *El*, the Canaanite term for God. God identifies himself to Abraham as *El Shaddai*, but the meaning of *Shaddai* is unclear today. Other names include *Elbethel* (God of Bethel, *Beth-el* itself meaning "House of God") and *El Ro'i* (God of Vision). Other names such as The Awesome One and God of the Fathers also appear in the Bible. In the Bible, God is most commonly referred to as the Lord (Adonai), the Lord God, or simply as God *(Elohim)*. All these names, including the word "God" itself, were considered to be honorary terms referring to His greatness, but not His real name. This name was uttered only once a year, by the high priest of the Temple on the day of fasting and prayer now known as Yom Kippur.

The ancient Hebrew tradition of not speaking the name of God carried over into a tradition of not writing it either. Jewish sacred texts represent the sacred name with a combination of four "y" and "h" sounds, giving rise to the mistaken idea that the ancient name for God was *Yahweh*. This word is read as Adonai. Some Jews go even further and avoid using any name for God conversationally, substituting ha-Shem, which simply means "the name," and sometimes writing God as "G-d." Traditionally, Torahs are stored in a special place rather than destroyed, because they contain representations of the name of God. Similarly, many Jews avoid putting even mass-produced copies of the Bible on the floor or treating them in any way that might scuff, tatter, or soil them. Others do not go to these lengths in speech or actions because, they point out, it is not the actual words on the page that are sacred but what is behind them, and in any event none of these terms are God's real name anyway.

Abraham and his followers wandered for years before finally settling permanently in Canaan, the area of today's Israel. During their wanderings Abraham's people came to be known as Hebrews. The origin of the name Hebrew is hotly debated by scholars today. Some say it is a descriptive term relating to a local word for the dust raised by nomads. Others say it came from the name of another wandering tribe, the Hapiru, with whom Abraham's tribe may have merged.

Abraham and his family journey to the Land of Canaan.

During those years of travel, his followers and his wealth grew, and during his lifetime he saw his people established as a powerful presence alongside the native Canaanites. Abraham's concept of monotheism, or belief in one God, also continued to evolve. The Canaanites worshiped many gods, most notably Baal and Astarte, and conceived of their gods similarly to the way the Mesopotamians did. Unlike his descendants generations later, Abraham did not concern himself with trying to convince or force the Canaanites to abandon their worship of Baal and other gods. He simply was sure he was right about the supreme power of his own god. Baal was either a lesser god or a false god, but either way, Baal was not his god. Concerned with the survival of his own people, he concentrated on living peaceably alongside his more numerous and better-established neighbors, content with what to him was the honor of worshiping the one true God.

Abraham's relationship with God was a very personal one. The Bible describes many occasions on which they talk directly to each other, and even times when God reveals Himself physically in Abraham's presence. The Bible tells of miracles and personal victories through which he came to understand more clearly the existence and nature of God. But it also tells of great challenges he faced to stay in the graces of such an all-powerful deity. Abraham, on several occasions, had to weigh unquestioning submission to the will of God against very human emotions of

The Women Behind the Men

Judaism is usually referred to as a patriarchal religion because, even though status as a Jew is conveyed through the mother, ancestry is traced through the men, men have greater authority, and men play most of the lead roles. Thus the contributions of all but a few of the Israelite women have been lost, but it is important to remember that they were there, raising families, supporting their husbands, and making great contributions to the evolution of Judaism.

Of Abraham's and Moses' wives, little is known except for a few stories that paint them as significant individuals with ideas of their own and the willingness to act on them. Sarah, Abraham's wife, was childless until the age of ninety, at which point, through the miraculous intervention of God, she bore a son, Isaac, who became the second Patriarch. However, in one of the saddest tales of human frailty in the Bible, in despair of her inability to conceive, she permitted her servant girl Hagar to sleep with Abraham so he could have some offspring. Sarah became consumed with jealousy when Hagar had a son, Ishmael, so she had them banished to the desert, presumably to die. Though they were rescued, the story points to the fact that people are often weak and make terrible mistakes, despite the clarity provided by religion about right and wrong.

Of Moses' wife Zipporah, even less is told. During the wanderings of the Hebrews in the desert after their escape from Egypt, Moses and Zipporah had a son whom Moses, for unknown reasons, had not circumcised as required by the covenant. Zipporah decided that if Moses would not do it himself, it was up to her, so she performed the circumcision herself. Both these stories suggest to modern readers how much is untold about daily life in the tents of the earliest Hebrew leaders, and how interesting the story of the strong women behind these men must be.

love and loyalty to kin. Abraham argued with God against destroying every last one of the Hebrew people in Sodom and Gomorrah when they had forgotten His ways, and he was put to the ultimate test when God told him to sacrifice his son Isaac to prove his devotion. At the moment Abraham lifted his knife to kill his child, he was stopped, because his willingness to choose God over even his own son had been proven.

The Covenant

This very personal relationship with God is at the heart of the development of the Hebrew faith in the era of the three Patriarchs (Abraham, his son Isaac, and Isaac's son Jacob), roughly 2000 B.C., when the idea of a covenant with

The Hebrews flee the destruction of Sodom and Gomorrah.

God began to evolve. The Biblical term "covenant" refers to a pact of mutual obligation between God and the Hebrew people, in which God agrees to be their God forever, to show them favor in His eyes, and never to abandon them, in exchange for their agreement to keep His laws and to have absolute faith in Him as the only God.

Sometimes, however, that faith was difficult for the Hebrews to keep. They endured many hardships that were difficult to reconcile with the idea of a loving and protecting God. However, unlike in Mesopotamian and Canaanite religions, the Bible makes a clear connection between their hardships and the weakness of their faith. Likewise, God is seen as a father figure who both loves and disciplines His children. The Hebrew God was one who identified right and wrong, and who dispensed divine justice even when it hurt. But He was also one who showed by His own actions the meaning of loyalty and faith by not abandoning His people even when they strayed.

This mutual contract to behave ethically is the greatest distinction between the Hebrew concept of God and any that had come before. As the Bible continues to recount the history of the Hebrew people,

the role of God as a moral force (including being bound by His own promises) and of the Hebrews as a people specially obligated by a covenant to live up to high standards of behavior become more and more the central focus of the faith that would become Judaism. What would also evolve was a clearer sense that there was only one God, the Lord God of the Hebrews, and only one way to be in His favor, by following the covenant. Baal and other objects of Canaanite worship became not just lesser deities with a limited degree of power, but nothing at all—just statues of stone or gold.

The Captivity in Egypt

Several hundred years passed between the time of the Patriarchs and the next critical time in the early history of the Hebrews, their enslavement in Egypt. In the intervening centuries, the Hebrews had grown in numbers and territory, especially as a result of the activities of the twelve sons of Abraham's grandson Jacob and their many offspring. Jacob himself played an essential role in the developing identity of the Hebrew people, for, as the Bible tells it, after an all-night struggle with an angel, Jacob was renamed "Israel," which means "he who struggles." From this point forward in the Bible, the descendants of the Patriarchs Abraham, Isaac, and Jacob are also commonly referred to as the children of Israel, or the Israelites.

Moses and the Covenant at Mount Sinai

By 1300 B.C. the Israelites had become slaves in Egypt for reasons that are not entirely clear. According to the Bible, as a means of ensuring that Hebrew numbers would not grow large enough to mount a rebellion, the ruler of Egypt, the pharaoh, ordered all male Hebrew babies killed at birth. One Hebrew mother hid her infant son in a basket along the banks of the Nile, where he was found by an Egyptian princess who wanted to keep the baby (whom she named Moses)

The pharaoh's daughter recovers Moses from a patch of reeds along the banks of the Nile.

as her own. A clever ruse by the baby's sister Miriam enabled his own mother to nurse him, so he was safely raised at home.

As a young adult, Moses observed the mistreatment of Hebrew slaves by a cruel overseer and became so angry that he killed the man. He was forced to flee for his life, and lived for many years in a desert region, where one day he witnessed a bush spontaneously burst into flame and heard the voice of God telling him to return to Egypt to free the Hebrews from captivity. At first reluctant to do so because he was "not a man of words," but "slow of speech and slow of tongue,"[4] he eventually went with his more articulate brother Aaron to try to convince the pharaoh.

After God empowered Moses to inflict a series of calamities such as plagues, infestations of locusts and frogs, and the killing of every first-born Egyptian son, the pharaoh relented and let the Hebrews leave. Changing his mind, he sent his army after them. They caught up to the Israelites in an area known as the Sea of Reeds. The Bible tells of the sea parting to let the Hebrews cross, then closing back in on the pharaoh's army. Today some scholars believe the Sea of Reeds was probably an area of tidal flats in eastern Egypt, and not the Red Sea, as the Biblical name is often translated. If so, the Hebrews would have been able pass at low tide on foot; but the Egyptians, following in their chariots, would have bogged down in the soft sand and been drowned by the incoming tide. In any event, the Hebrews were able to continue with no further Egyptian interference.

Once safely beyond the reach of the pharaoh, the Hebrews went on to reclaim the land in Canaan where Abraham had settled. But first, they had to travel across hundreds of miles of desert because powerful kingdoms blocked the more direct route. Their wanderings, which took many years, led them to the Sinai desert, where they camped at the base of Mount Sinai. There, according to the Bible, Moses and the Hebrew people had a series of encounters with God in which He laid down the Ten Commandments directly to the people and, speaking privately to Moses, issued hundreds of further directives and statements about diet, dress, worship, and other matters. The children of Israel then knew clearly what they must and must not do, and God once again promised to deliver them safely into

Moses commands the return of the Sea of Reeds (the Red Sea) after its parting.

Canaan and there to protect and sustain them as a people.

The Death of Moses

After the revelations at Mount Sinai, Moses and the Hebrews continued northward to Canaan. During their journey, said to have lasted forty years, the Israelites frustrated Moses by what historian Leo Trepp describes as their "fluctuations in commitment . . . [alternating] obedience with rebellion, trust with despair, unity with discord."[5] Their complaints, and Moses's typical response, have a very human and sometimes almost comically modern ring. For example, because they were unable to grow food, God supplied them each night with a miraculous substance called manna that dropped like dew on the ground, but after a while the people lost sight of the miracle and began to whine about how sick they were of having nothing else to eat. As the Hebrews bickered and fussed, Moses complained to God about what big babies they were. "Did I conceive all the people, did I bear them that you should say to me 'carry them in your bosom as a nurse carries an infant?'"[6]

Drained by the Israelites' apparent lack of faith in God's absolute promise to protect them and deliver them to the promised land, Moses began to tire of his role. When Moses sent ahead scouts, almost to a one they returned afraid of what lay ahead, and they spread doubt that the Israelites could ever succeed against such terrible odds. Almost in unison, the people loudly complained that they wished they had been left to die in Egypt, where at least there was food. Finally, in the wilderness of Zin, Moses's discouragement grew so great that God arranged for him to perform a miracle that would restore the people's faith. To answer their complaints about the lack of water, Moses was to point his staff at a rock a few yards away, and God would cause a spring to gush from the rock. Moses lost his temper when he faced the people, and in-

stead of just pointing the rod, he cried out, "Listen, you rebels, shall we get water for you out of a rock?"[7] and struck the ground twice. Water gushed out, as God had ordained, but God was angered by Moses's outburst, because it had made it unclear to the people that God and not Moses had the power to perform the miracle.

For that transgression, faithful Moses paid a large price. When, after forty years in the desert, the children of Israel finally stood overlooking the Jordan River and the promised land, Moses was not permitted to go any further with them. Instead, Joshua was chosen by God as the new leader. Though the Bible gives no reason for this choice, early Jewish scholars pointed out that Joshua was the only surviving Israelite scout who had consistently come back with glowing reports of a rich and fertile land ahead and no adversaries that could not be defeated. Joshua, therefore, perhaps was chosen because he had the optimism and faith to lead the new generation of Israelites. Nearing death, Moses reminded the Hebrews to "befriend the stranger, for you were strangers in the land of Egypt,"[8] and reviewed with them the requirements of the covenant. "And now, O Israel, what does the

Moses strikes a rock and brings water from its surface. This miracle renewed his followers' faith in God.

Lord demand of you? Only this: to revere the Lord your God, to walk only in His paths, to love Him and to serve the Lord your God with all your heart and soul, keeping the Lord's commandments and laws."[9]

These simple yet eloquent words reflect how consistently the Hebrew faith had evolved from Abraham's basic idea that the true God must be a supreme moral force capable of molding humans into their best selves and giving them the means to live together with dignity and respect. Though the Hebrews had failed much of the time to live up to the vision and faith of their great leaders, nevertheless a concept of themselves as a people united by a unique code of conduct, linked to a special relationship with the only true God, would continue to shape their identity in the years ahead.

chapter two

Life in the Promised Land

After the death of Moses, the Israelites, under the leadership of Joshua, crossed the Jordan River into Canaan. By this point they were a loose confederation of twelve tribes, descendants of the different sons of Jacob, each assigned a share of the land of Canaan. The conquest of Canaan may have been accomplished in several quick campaigns, as the Bible suggests, but it probably was a slower, messier process. According to historian Raymond P. Scheindlin, "Archaeological evidence is not conclusive, but it . . . suggests that some [Canaanite cities] were destroyed, rebuilt and redestroyed in the same period."[10] This suggests a series of battles rather than a few swift and conclusive victories, but in either case the end result was Israelite control of most of Canaan.

The sense of unity between the tribes began to weaken over time due to quarrels over territory and influence. The tribes lived independently and largely governed themselves. They came together occasionally in an institution called the Tent of Meeting, which had existed since the time of Moses, to discuss and resolve issues of common concern, but these meetings had become less and less important. At times, when a tribe felt particularly threatened, a flamboyant hero would emerge. These men and women were called Judges, although they functioned

Saul

When the people of Israel began clamoring for a king to protect them against the Philistines, the Prophet Samuel tried to talk them out of it, warning them that kings would inevitably become greedy and demanding, taking their sons and daughters as servants and keeping a portion of the profits from their lands. Nevertheless, they persisted, and God told a dubious Samuel to appoint a king. Saul's credentials for the role seem singularly undistinguished. He was tall and handsome, and he happened to show up in the right place at the right time, although he was only looking for a lost donkey. Soon after he was anointed king, his indecisiveness and his unwillingness to follow God's orders distressed Samuel and angered God, who ordered the Prophet to anoint another king.

Unknown to Saul, Samuel anointed David, a young shepherd, as the next king while Saul was still on the throne. David tried to please Saul by playing music for him and by serving heroically in his army, but Saul developed a jealousy that became murderous rage. Eventually Saul suffered a terrible military defeat to the Philistines, losing three sons in the battle. He committed suicide, a rarity in the Tanakh, and to complete his disgrace his decapitated body was impaled on the city wall and his head sent as a trophy on a tour of Philistine temples.

Today many readers of the story of Saul are struck by the descriptions of his personality. Saul was an intensely unhappy man, friendless and bitter. After a great military victory by David, "an evil spirit . . . gripped Saul, and he began to rave in the house" (1 Samuel 18:10). He threw a spear at David on two occasions, attempting to kill him, and similarly threatened his own son, Jonathan.

It is clear that Saul was suffering from a mental disorder that today might be better understood and perhaps treated, but to the people of the time, and to Saul himself, his affliction could only be attributed to unwelcome, and presumably terrifying, visits by an "evil spirit."

David plays a harp for king Saul.

more like warlords than as legal authorities. The best-known Judges are Gideon, Deborah, and Samson. But, according to famed writer Chaim Potok, "no judge succeeded in marshalling all the tribes for any one cause; either there was no cause strong enough or no judge so highly regarded."[11] He points out that the Israelite tribes had no standing army. "If you could not rally [the tribes] you failed; and the enemy plundered your crops, raided your villages, killed your people."[12]

The House of David

The cruel realities of life were underscored by the growing strength of the Philistines, a new and powerful people who settled on the southern coast of Canaan. The

David, who became one of history's great leaders, displays the head of Goliath to the Jews.

Philistines had large, well-equipped, and highly organized armies. In a devastating military defeat for the Israelites, the Philistines captured the sacred ark of the covenant, the lavishly decorated chest housing the original stones on which the Ten Commandments had been written. At that point several Israelite tribes decided it would be a good idea to unite under a king. They asked Samuel, a prophet who, according to the Bible, was able to speak with God, to determine God's will in the matter. Samuel, who was opposed to the Israelites having any other king but God, eventually went along when it was clear God approved of the idea. He anointed a warrior named Saul to be the first king of the Israelites. Saul was followed as king by a young warrior of humble origins who had made his reputation by killing the fearsome Philistine warrior Goliath and by slaying a large number of men in battle. His name was David, one of history's great leaders.

David's influence at the beginning was only in the south, primarily in the land of the tribe of Judah. Eventually he forged an alliance with the other tribes and became king of all Israel. He captured the city of Jerusalem from the Jebusites and, because of its central location, declared it the kingdom's capital. He set to work building the city and fortifying other towns to fend off would-be attackers. He conquered territory far beyond the traditional borders of Canaan in the regions of today's Syria, Lebanon, and Jordan. Under David, culture flourished as well. He is reputed to have been a fine musician and poet, and the authorship of many psalms is attributed to him. David's reign became known as the beginning of the Golden Age of Jewish history.

David's son and successor, Solomon, continued the Golden Age. Because David had provided the military strength that brought increased security and prosperity to the kingdom, Solomon was able to concentrate on promoting a great cultural legacy. He commissioned a written record of his father's life, which became the two biblical Books of Samuel, and sponsored the first attempt to write down the entire history of the Hebrews. That text has been lost but is known as a key source for the later compilers of the Torah. He also wanted public architecture to be suited to the greatness of the new kingdom. Chief among his accomplishments was the building of the Temple in Jerusalem. Observing that for cen-

The Prophets

The term "prophet" today refers to someone who has the ability to predict the future. The biblical prophets indeed were able to prophesy in that fashion, but their role is far larger than that. There are essentially two kinds of biblical prophets. Samuel is an example of the first kind. As a result of their ability to speak with God, they serve primarily as welcome or unwelcome advisers to kings. Samuel does not give speeches, he simply quietly reports and reflects the will of God. Elijah, whose story is told in the two books of Kings in the Tanakh, is less quiet but also fits in this mold as he rages at King Ahab about transgressing the will of God through his permissiveness toward his wicked wife Jezebel.

The second type, the literary prophets, were possessed by elaborate visions of what would happen in the future if the children of Israel did not mend their ways, or consequences to which their transgressions had already doomed them. The major prophets (so named because more sizable amounts of their writings have survived) are Jeremiah, Isaiah, and Ezekiel. To Isaiah is attributed the idea of the importance of inner virtue and good acts as a way of keeping the covenant. Jeremiah is renowned for his bleak visions of the loss of the promised land through the Jews' misbehavior. Ezekiel stressed individuals' responsibility for their own actions, and the ability of God to restore His people even after all hope seemed to be gone. The prophets were active, impassioned social critics who served as the conscience of a people, and still have that effect on those who read them today.

turies the Lord God of the Universe had been worshiped only at simple stone altars in the wilderness, Solomon decreed that a magnificent building be erected and that it be the only sanctioned place where the necessary sacrifices could be made.

The northern tribes endured heavy taxation to build the Temple and other public works in the south, projects they derived little benefit from. After Solomon died in 922 B.C. resentments boiled over against the favoritism shown by David and Solomon toward Judah, and the ten northern tribes broke away and formed a separate kingdom of Israel. The south became known as the Kingdom of Judah, and for several centuries the two kingdoms existed side by side. Though capable of cooperating in their mutual interests, for the most part they independently forged their own alliances with outsiders and tried to become as powerful as they could.

In the Path of Warring Empires

The Golden Age, however, was over. Much of the land David had added to his empire was lost. To the northeast the kingdom of Assyria was gathering strength, and to the southwest, Egypt was mobilizing to protect itself against an Assyrian bid for supremacy in the eastern Mediterranean. Caught between the two powers were the kingdoms of Israel and Judah.

In 745 B.C. a new, ruthless, and very effective ruler, Tiglath-pileser III, took over the throne of Assyria. Within less than ten years Tiglath-pileser was demanding tribute money from Israel, in essence a bribe to keep Assyria from invading. Israel tried to get Judah to agree to join an alliance of smaller nations of the region to fight off Assyria, but Ahaz, the king of Judah, refused. Angered, Israel invaded Judah. In response, Ahaz made a tactical decision that would have a major effect on subsequent Jewish history—he asked Tiglath-

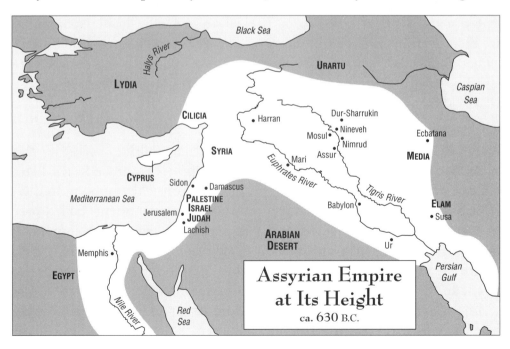

Assyrian Empire at Its Height
ca. 630 B.C.

pileser for his help. Happy to oblige, the Assyrians marched into Israel, deposed the king, and installed another monarch they thought they could more easily control. This "puppet king," Hoshea, proved unreliable, however, and tried to form an alliance with Egypt to push out the Assyrians. When Tiglath-pileser's successor, Shalmaneser V, heard of this, he attacked again, overthrew the monarchy of Israel altogether, and deported much of the population, thereby ending the two-hundred-year history of the Kingdom of Israel.

Judah was to suffer the same fate several hundred years later, when Assyria had been replaced by Babylonia as the dominant power in the region. Egypt remained the great adversary, and Judah, as before, was caught in the middle. In 597 B.C. King Zedekiah of Judah broke an oath of loyalty to the Babylonian king Nebuchadnezzar II. Nebuchadnezzar promptly invaded Judah and besieged Jerusalem. Leaving Judah only long enough to continue to Egypt and defeat it in battle, Nebuchadnezzar returned and overran Jerusalem in 587 B.C. The Temple and the other great architecture of the Solomonic era were destroyed, the monarchy was overthrown, and much of the population was de-ported to Bablylon, thus beginning the period known as the Babylonian captivity.

The Babylonian Captivity

Not all the Israelites were sent off to Babylonia, but the vast majority of the skilled and educated ones were, leaving behind a dramatically weakened population. Four hundred years before, the monarchy in Judah had risen to a peak with David and Solomon, and the idea of a promised land seemed to have been realized, only to disappear at the hands of powerful foreigners. Prophets such as Jeremiah were quick to say that God's promise to the Hebrew people was fulfilled by both the rise and the fall of Judah, for the curses of not following God's laws were as much part of the covenant as its blessings. As the remaining Israelites cleared the ruins of the Temple and the others made the long trek to Babylonia, a new understanding of the covenant, born of their defeat, began to take shape. Over time, it would become the foundation of the religion of Judaism as it is known today.

In the words of historian Raymond P. Scheindlin, the deported Israelites "took the memory of the kingdom with them into exile, and there they nourished themselves on the dream that it would ultimately be restored to the glory of its early days."[13] "By the rivers of Babylon/there we sat and wept/as we thought of Zion," Psalm 137 says, followed by a promise still echoed by Jews today: "If ever I forget you, O Jerusalem, let my right hand wither/Let my tongue stick to my palate if I cease to think of you."[14] From this was born what is often referred to as the messianic idea, a belief of a captive people that a time would come when Jerusalem, symbol of the covenant, would be restored through an "anointed one," or messiah. Scheindlin points out that

"along with the principle of monotheism, the messianic dream was to become one of the defining features of Judaism."[15]

Another feature of Judaism would also begin to emerge during the Babylonian captivity. Because the religion of the children of Israel had revolved around priests and sacrifices, as commanded by God in Sinai, once the Temple was destroyed, there was no way to continue to observe the covenant as before. A new concept emerged, that the faith could be kept through direct study and compliance with the Torah. Torah study itself was not only a demonstration of obedience and commitment to God in

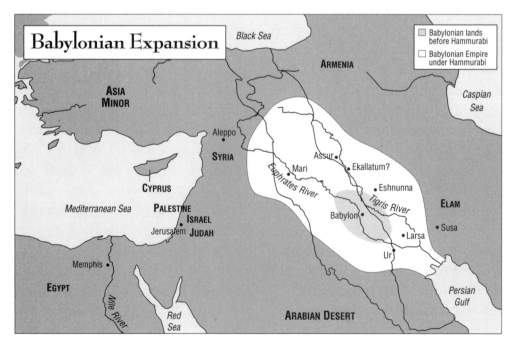

The army of Cyrus of Persia marches into Babylon. Cyrus's invasion ended the Babylonian captivity.

the same way symbolic sacrifices of animals and grain had been, but it would also help the rabbis, religious scholars and leaders, figure out ways the covenant could be kept in drastically changed times. Judaism became, from that point forward, increasingly characterized by rabbis—teachers and scholars moved by love of God and Torah—rather than by a hereditary class of priests deemed to have special powers and influence with God.

Regathering in Judea

The Babylonian captivity actually did not last very long. In 539 B.C.

Cyrus of Persia captured both Babylonia and Judah, which was renamed Judea. From this point forward the children of Israel began to be known as Jews, from the word Judea. Cyrus's approach to conquered people was radically different from what had come before or would follow. He recognized that his territorial gains would be more secure if he could gain conquered peoples' loyalty, so instead of deporting captives or destroying the important symbols of their culture such as places of worship, he encouraged conquered people to continue with their lives as before. In fact, he encouraged the Babylonian Jews to return to Jerusalem and even funded the restoration of the Temple, which was rededicated in 515 B.C. under Cyrus's heir, Darius I.

Many Jews in Babylon did not return, however, because they had prospered there, and they were reluctant to leave what had become comfortable lives and a higher standard of living than before. They remained loyal and committed Jews, however, establishing, along with a similar community in Egypt, one of the most brilliant and remarkable spiritual, intellectual, and cultural communities in Judaism's long history. These communities had actually grown so extensively that historians believe that by the third century B.C. there were more Jews living outside Judea than in it. Judea was nevertheless the spiritual home of all the Jews, and those who lived elsewhere sent money for the upkeep of the Temple and its rituals, and made reference to it in their prayers.

In Judea, the two centuries of Persian domination were a time of religious renewal, encouraged by the Persians to the extent that the prophet Ezra was officially commissioned by the Persian emperor to make the Torah the law of the land. The book of Ezra recounts the ceremony at the Temple where

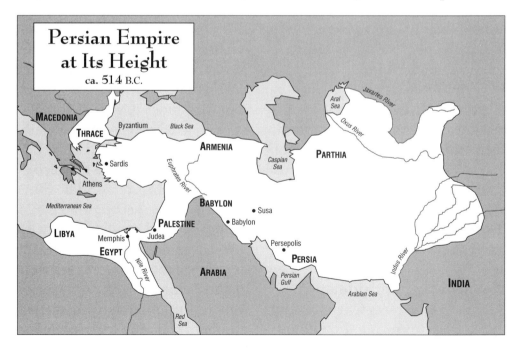

Persian Empire at Its Height
ca. 514 B.C.

MACEDONIA
THRACE
Byzantium
Black Sea
Sardis
Athens
Mediterranean Sea
ARMENIA
Caspian Sea
PARTHIA
Aral Sea
Jaxartes River
Oxus River
Euphrates River
BABYLON
Susa
Babylon
LIBYA
PALESTINE
Memphis
Judea
EGYPT
Nile River
Persepolis
PERSIA
Persian Gulf
ARABIA
Indus River
Arabian Sea
INDIA
Red Sea

Ezra officially read the Torah in public to symbolize this beginning. Under Ezra and a Jewish governor, Nehemiah, a new spirit of commitment to the laws of the Torah emerged. Holidays began to be celebrated as the Torah decreed; the restored Temple became once again the center of worship; and marriage and commerce with non-Jews were actively discouraged to keep foreign ideas and blood out of the Jewish community.

Hellenization

All empires fall, however. In 332 B.C., under Alexander the Great, the new superpower, Greece, conquered Egypt and much of the Middle East, including Judea. According to Raymond P. Scheindlin, "Jews would be both fascinated and repelled by this culture for centuries to come; even those who resisted it most bitterly could hardly escape its influence."[16] Greek art, architecture, music, literature, political organization, and social structure all dazzled the Judeans, who, though they had a glorious Temple, could not match in their daily lives the intellectual and aesthetic advances of the Greeks. Many Jews in Judea and the other communities in the Greek Empire, such as Alexandria in Egypt, strove to be as much like

the Greeks as possible. Egyptian Jews read a Torah translated into Greek because they no longer bothered to learn Hebrew. Some Judean Jews even stopped circumcising their sons because Greek athletic competitions were done in the nude, and they wanted their bodies to look more Greek. Such actions enraged other Jews, for they struck at the heart of what Jews considered sacred—the Torah, and the mark of the covenant in the flesh of Jewish men. To abandon their God in favor of a culture that still worshiped many gods and demanded that their emperor be treated as a living god was a horror beyond imagination for these Jews, and a terrible comedown after the years of Persian tolerance and support.

The Greek period, under a dynasty known as the Seleucids, therefore, was characterized by social upheaval and unrest. As opposition to the influence of the Greeks became more widespread and pronounced, the Greek reaction became more and more repressive. Antiochus IV Epiphanes became the Greek emperor in 175 B.C. The antithesis of the Persian Cyrus, Antiochus wanted to create one unified Greek culture in his entire empire. He tried to force subject

Alexander the Great triumphantly enters Babylon. Alexander brought Greek culture to the Jews.

people to adopt Greek education, fashion, and religious practices. Many in Judea welcomed the idea of using Greek power to destroy Hebrew customs they considered rigid, confining, and outdated; in fact, one member of the Judean social elite, Joshua, who took the Greek name Jason, was able to bribe Antiochus to make him high priest on the promise of Hellenizing (making Greek) the practices of the Temple. He was succeeded by Menelaus, who went even further by selling the Temple vessels and allowing Antiochus's soldiers to plunder the Temple.

Copies of the Torah were destroyed, circumcision was made illegal, and celebrations of Jewish festivals were forbidden under Antiochus. In 167 B.C. the Temple was officially dedicated as a shrine to the Greek gods, and a pig was sacrificed on its altar—a deliberate outrage because pork is a food forbidden by the covenant. With Antiochus, the Jews experienced persecution for their Jewishness for the first time in history. Previously the Jews' status had been determined simply by whether they were conqueror or conquered. From this point on, however, they began to experience a disrespect for their faith that would have increasingly tragic consequences in the centuries ahead.

As the Seleucid dynasty's treatment of the Jews became more and more demeaning, opposition grew more passionate. One family of priests, the Maccabees, were particularly associated with this opposition. The father, Mattathias, and his five sons initiated a campaign against the Seleucids focused on harassing soldiers and destroying pagan altars. The most famous of his sons, Judah, was able to recapture the Temple in 164 B.C. and restore it to proper Jewish use, an achievement celebrated in the festival of Hanukkah. Subsequent generations of Maccabees, lacking this initial passion, founded their short-lived Hasmonaean dynasty by agreeing not to cause trouble for the Seleucids in exchange for greater autonomy, especially in religious matters.

Roman Occupation

The end eventually came for the Seleucids when in 63 B.C. the Roman Empire took control of Judea, installing Herod as king in 37 B.C. Herod was neither Judean nor Roman, though he was a Jew. He was, in the words of Raymond P. Scheindlin, "a ruthless manipulator, a brilliant diplomat, and large

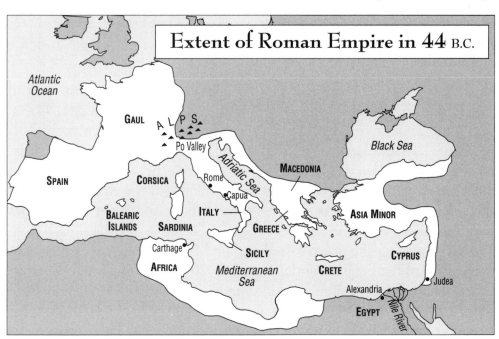

Extent of Roman Empire in 44 B.C.

Atlantic Ocean

GAUL

ALPS

Po Valley

Black Sea

SPAIN

CORSICA

Rome

MACEDONIA

Adriatic Sea

Capua

BALEARIC ISLANDS

SARDINIA

ITALY

GREECE

ASIA MINOR

Carthage

SICILY

CYPRUS

AFRICA

CRETE

Mediterranean Sea

Alexandria

Judea

EGYPT

Nile River

Jesus and the Jews

The Roman occupation of the region they called Judea was a particularly oppressive one. Civil rights were entirely absent. Troublemakers were tortured and often killed publicly as deterrents to others. The Temple was desecrated with pagan symbols. In this environment, it is no surprise that the suffering Jews looked to the sacred texts of their prophets for words of consolation. In them were found visions of a time when all would be set right and they would live as God intended, free from oppression and in complete and joyful submission to God's will. Because some of these visions referred to an "anointed one" or "messiah" ("mashiach" in Hebrew), many people thought a specific individual would come, perhaps an avenging angel who would make war on oppressors with all the force of God. Or perhaps, some thought, the messiah might take some other form, even that of a man.

To a small group of Jews, Jesus of Nazareth was the long awaited Messiah. These Jews, known as Nazarenes, became the first proponents of what would in time become a new faith, Christianity. Unlike some other preachers of that and other eras, Jesus himself, according to the Gospels, never publicly claimed to be the Messiah. Many around him believed he was, and that was enough to bring him to the attention of the Roman authorities. He was arrested and tortured by Romans and eventually became one of many during that era to be crucified, a

scale personality,"[17] worthy of the title Herod the Great by which he is commonly known. Herod built new cities such as Caesarea, an important new port on the Mediterranean, as well as fortresses such as the one at Masada. Most important to the Jews, he rebuilt the Temple, replacing the one restored in the time of the Persians and pillaged and defiled by the Greeks, with one even more magnificent than that built by Solomon.

Another King Herod, Herod Antipas, followed Herod the Great, ruling from 4 B.C. to A.D. 39. It is this Herod who is familiar to Christians from the story of Jesus. During his reign, the Roman emperor decided to divide the empire into administrative provinces, each to be ruled by a procurator, a governor loyal to the Romans. The most famous of these procurators is Pontius Pilate, who gave the order for Jesus' crucifixion. These procurators

horrifying and excruciatingly painful death intended to symbolize the powerlessness of those who opposed the Romans. For centuries Jews suffered violent and often deadly anti-Semitic attacks because they, rather than the Roman authorities, were accused of being responsible for the death of Jesus; but Pope John Paul II has declared that the church was wrong to have promoted that idea.

Jews today see Jesus' teachings as generally consistent with the Judaism of the time but of far less importance philosophically than those of several other rabbis in the same period, including Hillel and Shammai, whose names have been eclipsed, at least among Christians, by their far more famous contemporary.

Roman guards place a crown of thorns on Jesus' head. The Romans devised many cruel punishments for those who opposed them.

had a significant effect on the lives of the Jews; they were responsible for collecting the astronomical taxes required for the upkeep of the Roman army and administration, and for keeping order, which was often done brutally.

Tensions continued to rise. A secret group of Jewish zealots, known as *sicarii* or "daggermen," began to intimidate Romans and their Jewish collaborators by knifing them as they passed on the streets.

Spontaneous protests and clashes with Roman soldiers frequently became violent. In A.D. 66 the situation came to a head when the procurator Florus needed money and decided to confiscate some of the Temple treasures. A large-scale revolt followed.

The Jews Fight Back

Despite the superior might of the Romans, the Jewish revolt lasted four years. It was not until A.D. 70

that the Romans concentrated their efforts to end it. With a newly focused Roman Legion behind him, the general Titus quickly conquered Jerusalem and destroyed the Temple. When a few *sicarii* took refuge at Herod's old fortress at Masada, the Romans built a massive ramp up the side of the high cliffs on which Masada is perched. When they finally broke down the gates of the fortress they discovered everyone inside had committed suicide rather than be taken captive.

The punitive measures that followed the Great Revolt were as shocking as its dramatic climax of suicides at Masada. According to historian Leo Trepp, "After the defeat of the rebels, the Romans razed cities, devastated the land, carried tens of thousands of Jews into slavery, dispossessed Jewish farmers who had remained, settled non-Jewish colonists on their farms, and imposed crushing taxes on the Jewish population."[18] Much of the Jewish population left Judea, either by force or because there was nothing left to sustain them there.

Some stayed behind, however, and because they had so thoroughly defeated the Jews, the Romans thought there was no danger in letting the faith continue to be practiced. One religious leader,

Rabbi Johanan, founded a small academy of Jewish learning, called the Sanhedrin, formerly a Temple-based institution that had ceased to function when the Temple was destroyed. The new Sanhedrin was important because it served as the seat of religious authority once the Temple was gone.

In time, the Jews of Judea rebounded sufficiently from their defeat to begin to rebel again, especially when the Roman emperor went back on a promise to rebuild the Temple and decided to make Jerusalem a modern Roman city. In A.D. 132 the Jews revolted again over the issues of the remodeling of Jerusalem and a new ban on circumcision. The leader of the revolt was a rabbi named Simon Ben-Kosiba, who was eventually killed by the Romans in A.D. 135. Hailed as a hero, he was later renamed Bar Kokhba (Son of the Star) by his admirers, and his insurrection is known as the Bar Kokhba revolt.

The Diaspora

After brutally suppressing the Bar Kokhba revolt, the Romans ceased all tolerance of the practice of Judaism. Religious observance was outlawed, many rabbis endured death by torture at public ceremonies, thousands of Jews were enslaved, and close to a million were killed. In the final indignity, the city of Jerusalem was renamed Aelia Capitolina in honor of its new, totally Roman identity, and Judea was itself renamed Palestine. Though a few Jews remained in a land that no longer bore their name, the promised land seemed to be irrevocably lost.

The dispersal of the Jewish people, an ongoing historical event sometimes referred to as the Diaspora, had begun with the Assyrians seven hundred years before, but Jews of the Diaspora had always known where the center of the Jewish faith was. In the aftermath of the crushed Bar Kokhba revolt, the identity of Jews changed. There was no longer a center, no longer a home except in the hearts and the imagination—a situation that would endure for almost two thousand years. Jews would have to establish new centers of Judaism wherever they went. If Judaism were to survive, it would have to be kept alive not in the land of the covenant, but in Jewish communities wherever they might be.

chapter | three

Jews and Their Communities

The Romans must have thought that in destroying the Temple they could destroy Judaism. After all, according to Rabbi Stephen M. Wylen, "Every religion in the world had temples for sacrifice and a priesthood to officiate in the temples. There was no religion without sacrifice."[19] The Romans were wrong. By the time of the destruction of the Second Temple in A.D. 70, Jews had already lived far from Palestine for hundreds of years, in strong and thriving communities in Babylon, Egypt, and elsewhere. For a period of time even in Palestine, they had lived without a Temple. During this time, the nature of Judaism had changed in a way that made it not only able to survive the loss of the Second Temple, but actually, some scholars argue, to profit as a faith because of it. The moral authority of the Temple-based priesthood had been severely undermined by collaboration with the Romans. Additionally, the fact that the role of priest was a hereditary one meant that many priests were simply not suited to the role because they lacked true piety and religious commitment. The new Sanhedrin established by Johanan represented a positive development for post-Temple Judaism because it was an institution where scholarship and intellect were revered and the leaders were generally sincere men of faith.

The Sanhedrin's essential message was that God, in the words of the Prophet Hosea, wanted from His people, "goodness, not sacrifice/ Obedience to God rather than burnt offerings."[20] This simple statement represents a profound shift in the Jews' concept of the covenant, for in this view it could be kept, wherever Jews were, by following the laws of the Torah. This development laid the groundwork for Judaism today. As Jews spread out over the centuries to become usually a small minority in whatever country or empire became home, they were bound to each other by the Torah, and by the evolving institutions of the synagogue and the yeshiva, or study center. Despite the diversity that evolved over the centuries in Jewish communities around the world, the essential practices and views that marked one as a Jew remained remarkably similar. Unfortunately, persecution for sticking to their distinct culture and faith followed Jews everywhere as well. Yet despite the difficulties inherent in being Jewish, the practice of Judaism has survived uninterrupted for four millenia.

Jews in the Middle Ages

After the dispersal from Palestine, or the Diaspora, Jews could be found almost everywhere in the world. In the medieval era they often played a significant role in the intellectual and cultural history of their adopted homes. Two Jewish communities, one in Spain and one in Poland, stand out in this respect. Between the eighth and thirteenth centuries, Muslims ruled Spain. It was a period of great cultural advances, and for the Jews, a time in which they were treated with an unusual level of freedom and civil rights. As *dhimmis,* or protected subjects, Jews had the right to practice their faith, although they were heavily taxed for the privilege. They also had other restrictions designed to show their subordinate status, such as prohibitions (often ignored) on building new synagogues or repairing old ones. As Raymond P. Scheindlin points out, "while Jews may have been tolerated by Islam, they were nevertheless regarded as alien."[21] However, despite the Jews' status as outsiders, the Arab upper class was sophisticated and well educated enough to welcome Jewish intellectuals, poets, and artists. Jews such as Hasdai Ibn-Shaprut and Samuel ha-Nasid even became chief advisers to Muslim rulers, and in that status were able to use their influence to keep relations positive between Arabs and Jews.

When the Almohad sect of Muslims took power in the early twelfth century, Jews began to lose the prestigious positions they had gained in the Muslim courts and found it more difficult to make a living and observe Jewish ways at home. However, the Muslim empire in Spain was quickly falling to Christian forces from the north. Led by the king of Castile, the Christian conquest at first seemed promising for Jews, for those who had fled north were being treated well, in contrast to their usual experience in Christian-dominated lands. However, this tolerance did not last. An outbreak of the Black Death, bubonic plague, struck Europe and in a society ignorant of the causes of disease, the Church focused attention off its own helplessness and onto the Jews, who were said to be poisoning wells and otherwise causing the epidemic. Blaming Jews for catastrophes was nothing new. The "blood libel" was already popular in Europe, an accusation that Christian murder victims had been killed by Jews who needed their blood to make matzo, the special bread of Passover.

The Black Death was not the only cause of negative attention focused on the Jews. The Crusades, "holy wars" to free Palestine from

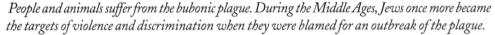

People and animals suffer from the bubonic plague. During the Middle Ages, Jews once more became the targets of violence and discrimination when they were blamed for an outbreak of the plague.

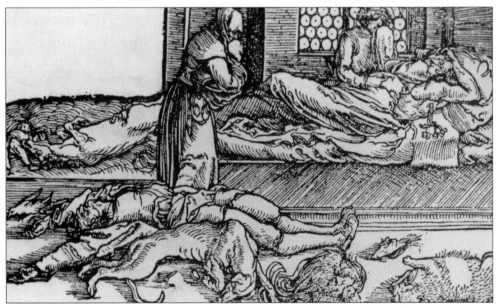

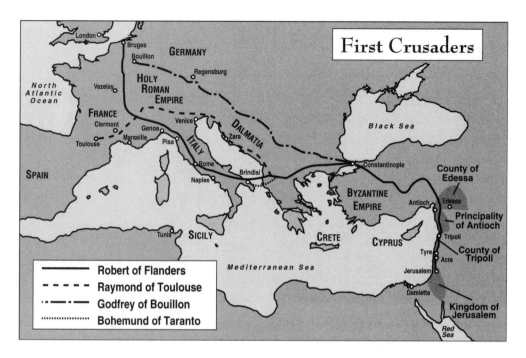

First Crusaders

Legend:
— Robert of Flanders
- - - Raymond of Toulouse
-·-·- Godfrey of Bouillon
·········· Bohemund of Taranto

Muslim conquerors, were not directly focused against the Jews, but created a backlash against them nevertheless. As Christians became absorbed by what was presented as a sacred mission against Muslims, they extended their zeal to the other non-Christian group in their midst, the Jews. Convinced of their religious and spiritual superiority, the Christians of Spain and other parts of Europe felt justified in turning against their Jewish neighbors for what Christians perceived as the supreme insult, the Jews' rejection of Jesus as the messiah.

By the early fifteenth century Jews were subject to mob violence and open discrimination in Spain. Many left for regions controlled by Muslims, including Palestine, bringing their advanced Sephardic (from Sepharadh, the Hebrew word for Spain) culture with them. Others were subject to mass conversion, sometimes directly against their will, and sometimes only after immense pressure. Some "New Christians," or conversos, embraced the new faith, but many continued to practice Judaism secretly. In 1480 the conversos became subject to one of the cruelest institutions in medieval times, the Inquisition. The Inquisition was designed to root out heresy among Christians. Jews were not subject to it because they were

A soldier tortures a Jewish prisoner during the Spanish Inquisition. Many Jews were tortured and killed for secretly practicing their faith.

not Christian, but conversos were special targets. Many were tortured into confessing they were still Jews at heart, after which they were burned at the stake in great public spectacles. Finally, in 1492 King Ferdinand and Queen Isabella signed an edict expelling all Jews from Spain. The golden age of Spanish Jewry was at an end.

The Jews of Poland

Jews in France, Germany, and other parts of Europe were also persecuted for similar reasons dur-ing medieval times. As a result, many Jews left their homes and went east. Raymond P. Scheindlin writes that in fact, "because of their high education level, their skills, and their international busi-ness connections . . . the kings and nobles of Poland were encourag-ing the Ashkenazic [European] Jews to settle in their territories."[22] By 1600, Jews were thriving in Poland and elsewhere in eastern Europe, living as farmers, skilled artisans, merchants, and also as part of the Polish bureaucracy, handling government matters such as tax collection, much as their Sephardic counterparts had done for centuries among the Muslims.

Jews remained set apart in their own communities, often by choice at this time. They continued to speak their own language, a combination of the German most of them had spoken before immigration, with Slavic and Hebrew elements. This language became known as Yiddish, one of the great unifying elements among eastern European Jews. There were occasional serious outbreaks of anti-Semitism, most notably the slaughter of Jews by Ukrainian cossacks in the mid-1600s, which caused many Jews to return to western Europe. Also, the Protestant Reformation and the Catholic response, known as the Counter-Reformation, were unfavorable developments for Jews all over Europe, because the struggle between the two branches of Christianity became focused around what was or was not religious deviancy. In the eyes of zealous Protestants and Catholics alike, Jews were the most notable of deviants.

Nevertheless, Jewish culture thrived in eastern Europe. Even when the lands of eastern Poland became part of Russia in the 1770s,

and Russian intolerance led to restrictions on where Jews could live, they developed a vibrant Ashkenazic culture in the shtetls, or Jewish villages, of a region known as the Pale of Settlement. It was in this region that one of the most important developments in Judaism, Hasidism, evolved in the early 1700s as a reaction to the increasingly complex and intellectual approach of rabbis to the faith. Founded by Ba'al Shem Tov, Hasidism emphasizes direct experience of the divine through focused contemplation that was "bound to fill the heart with religious joy and enthusiasm."[23]

Crowding Jews into towns within a confined area contributed to the development of a unique Jewish way of life, but it also made Jews more vulnerable to attack. In the 1880s the Russian army swept through the Pale of Settlement on horseback, slaughtering whole communities of Jews based on rumors of their political involvement in plots against the czar, Alexander III. As with the medieval blood libel, the illogic of the claim that poor Jews in remote areas could manage to assassinate a czar living under heavy guard in a faraway palace was disregarded. Jews began to emigrate to western Europe and the United States in large

The Hasidim

In mid-eighteenth century Poland, a movement known as Hasidism arose in reaction to the studious, rabbinical Judaism of the time. Its founder, Israel ben Eliezer (ca. 1700–1760), also known as Ba'al Shem Tov (Master of the Good Name of God), believed that God could best be worshipped not by intellectual study or by proliferation of texts such as the Talmudic commentaries, but by joy in being part of his creation. In the words of Leo Trepp, in *A History of the Jewish Experience*, to the practitioners of Hasidism,

> "Joy—not simple enjoyment but the delight that comes from doing everything for God—released the sparks of God's presence and therefore permeated every act, be it eating, drinking, or manual labor, or pipe smoking, which the Baal Shem liked."

Jews, according to the Ba'al Shem Tov, were God's agents on earth, and they should strive to maintain a personal feeling of cleaving to God by acting with *kavanah,* or intent. This could be done by ecstatic experiences such as dancing and praying with abandon, swaying back and forth, and letting prayer itself become an emotional high.

The Hasidic rebbe (so called because rabbi was a word reserved for the conventionally trained rabbis of the time) was often a charismatic figure. Their disciples flocked to spend the Sabbath and holidays with them, treating even a moment's audience in a receiving line as an intense spiritual experience. Rebbes had miracles attributed to them, and their every word was treated as extraordinarily insightful.

Negative reaction to the Hasidim was very strong among conventional rabbis, and a countermovement, called the Mitnagdim, evolved to quash the movement. However, the Hasidim and Mitnagdim soon recognized that the greater threat to both was Reform Judaism. A fusion of the views of both occurred, and Hasidic Jews became more Torah oriented, focusing their joy on close observance of Jewish law. Ironically, what had once been the most radical form of Judaism became one of the most traditional. Today the extremely observant Chabad movement, an acronym formed from the first Hebrew letters in the words "wisdom, understanding, and knowledge," is the locus of Hasidic Judaism in the United States.

Russian police look on as Jews are assaulted during a pogrom in Kiev, Ukraine, in the 1880s.

numbers in this era, not just from fear of these violent attacks, known as pogroms, but also from the realization that their options were hopelessly limited by life within the Pale. As tales of immigrant success began to filter back, emigration from all over eastern Europe reached flood levels, changing forever the context and culture of Jewish life not just for those who left their eastern European roots behind, but also for those whose worlds they entered.

Jewish Life in the Cities of Europe

The shtetl Jews relocated primarily in cities. Conditions varied from place to place, but in some cases the Jews faced discrimination and hardship similar to what they had left behind. Since the 1500s many European Jews had been forced to live in ghettos, walled cities within a city where Jews were locked in at night and residents could go in and out only at the will of the local government.

Living conditions were usually horrible due to lack of sanitation and overcrowding.

Not all cities had ghettos, though many had demeaning customs such as tolls to pass through the city gates for any creature with a cloven hoof, which was defined as including "cattle and Jews,"[24] a reference to the belief that the devil had such a feature. In Paris and other northern European cities, Jews were more able to function within the larger society. In Amsterdam, for example, Jews flourished as doctors, government officials, lawyers, and merchants, contributing culturally and intellectually to the extent that Amsterdam was sometimes called "the Dutch Jerusalem."[25] During the nineteenth century Jews gradually gained full civil rights all over Europe. The French emperor Napoléon declared that Jews were French by nationality and Jewish only by religion. This enabled Jews, who to that point had been treated as resident aliens, to be French citizens on an equal basis. It was, according to historian Raymond P. Scheindlin, "a decisive moment in the history of Judaism,"[26] because for the first time the implication was clear that Jews were no longer to be viewed as a separate people. As Napoléon's conquest of Europe

spread, this change in perception spread with it.

For many European Jews this was a positive development, for it reflected how they already saw themselves. To them, their community was their city, and though many retained Jewish customs at home and worshiped in synagogues, they tried otherwise to fit in with the Christian majority. Many Jews sent their children to the same schools as Christians, did not give them a supplementary Jewish education, and drifted away from formal observance of the faith. Some families such as the Rothschilds and Oppenheimers amassed great wealth, but the typical western European Jew strove only to be solidly in the middle class through acquiring a profession and trying to fit within the Christian communities of Europe. Imperial proclamations notwithstanding, the public did not necessarily view Jews as full citizens, however, and rampant anti-Semitism was still a deeply ingrained aspect of society.

Though applauding the improvement in their legal status, Jewish leaders were dismayed at the erosion of the practice of Judaism in nineteenth-century Europe. They perceived as a real risk that what Babylonians, Romans, Inquisitors, and other persecutors had failed to do might be brought about from within, as Jews quietly seemed to be assimilating themselves out of existence. From this situation in Germany emerged the Reform movement, which tried to reconcile the realities of the modern world with the ancient Jewish faith and thus bring Jews back into their religious community. Reform congregations removed rituals or practices that made Jews feel alien and unnecessarily different from their Christian neighbors. They relaxed dietary laws and prohibitions against intermarriage, and moved away from using Hebrew in worship. Reform Jews worshiped in buildings called temples rather than synagogues to suggest that Jews had replaced the dream of a restored temple in Jerusalem as a symbol of a united Jewish people with centers of worship established in their own communities. Thus, Reform Judaism played an important role in preserving the religion during a period of adjustment to a new, strongly nationalistic world.

Jews in America

For the Jews of eastern Europe, assimilation was not an option, and pogroms and other forms of anti-Semitism made life precarious and the future dim. Immigration seemed the best solution, and though many simply moved west to Vienna, Berlin, Paris, and other cities, some went straight to America. But Jewish immigration was not a new phenomenon. In fact the first Jews came from Holland by way of Brazil as early as 1654. The Newport Synagogue in Rhode Island dates from 1763, attesting to the presence of a Jewish community in the colonies before the American Revolution. Jewish numbers were very small, probably no more than two thousand altogether in the thirteen colonies. By the 1830s a substantial number of German immigrants began to arrive, some fleeing persecution but others simply attracted by the chance of owning land and having great social mobility within which to prosper financially. Their skills as traders and merchants brought them success, though few could match the achievement of Levi Strauss, a Jew who arrived in San Francisco as a tent maker for prospectors and ended up being a mine owner and millionaire, immortalized today on the backs of millions of pairs of jeans.

In the 1880s huge waves of eastern European immigrants began to

The Holocaust

Among the most tragic Jewish communities in history were the ones created by the Nazis during World War II in the ghettos, camps, and hiding places where Jews, debilitated by hunger, disease, and despair, crowded together. Altogether, more than 6 million Jews lost their lives, a number in excess of the entire population of Jews in the United States today. It was to be the "Final Solution" to what Adolf Hitler and the Nazi Party saw as the problem caused by the mere existence of Jews in the world. More than a third of the world's Jews died in the Holocaust, and three-quarters of the Jews of Europe. In Poland, which before the war had been home to 3 million Jews, only seventy thousand survived. Today Poland, which once served as the home of nearly 40 percent of the world's Jews and was its most vibrant center of culture, has only a few thousand. In a final horror, many Polish death camp survivors were killed by their anti-Semitic neighbors when they tried to return home, and at that point most remaining Jews decided to emigrate to Israel or elsewhere.

Despite the unrelenting horror of the camps, they did indeed serve as communities. In them, Jews struggled to continue to perform mitzvot such as charity and religious observance, and though many lost their faith, many others did not, and murmured prayers could still be heard and furtive minyans attended. Survivors of the camps describe heroic efforts to save each other from being selected to die, tendernesses performed toward those sick and dying of starvation and disease, and even occasional moments of joy, such as weddings. Though the Nazis

did everything they could to reduce them to the status of animals, the Jews kept their dignity of spirit even when all other vestiges of dignity were gone. In the end, the living skeletons liberated from the camps did not look as if they had won a war, but indeed, in a very real sense they had.

Emaciated from starvation, Holocaust victims are heaped together.

Russian Jewish refugees sail past the Statue of Liberty on their way to America.

arrive, and though the now well-assimilated and successful German Jews found the immigrants' very traditional Jewish lifestyle a bit of an embarrassment, they saw the key to a continued respected place for Jews in American society as hinging on how successfully these Jews could be Americanized. However, the new Jewish immigrants, though anxious to succeed in America, were not willing to forego their traditional ways, and although they lived in poverty, crammed into tenements in large cities, they established vibrant communities characterized by Yiddish conversations, Orthodox practices, and American hopes. These new immigrants revitalized Judaism in the

United States. Charitable organizations, schools to train rabbis, and political action groups began to form, and the Jewish presence in the United States began to be more noticeable and distinct.

Typically, the more Jews were noticed, the stronger was the reaction against them. For example, blatantly manipulated quotas to limit Jewish immigration to the United States slowed their exodus out of Europe just as the Nazis were coming to power in Germany. Moreover, many scholars have pointed out that America might have played a bigger role in preventing, minimizing, or ending the Holocaust. Even so, Jews in the United States have flourished in the open-minded American environment, and this has enabled them to reach out over the generations to help their fellow Jews in less secure situations around the world.

Today there are more Jews in New York than there are in Tel Aviv, the largest city in Israel, and Los Angeles has a larger Jewish population than either Jerusalem or Haifa, Israel's second and third largest cities. Jews routinely rise to the tops of corporations and achieve distinctions such as university professorships that were once barred to them in more anti-Semitic times.

One sign of the changing times was the Democrat's choice of Senator Joseph Lieberman as the vice presidential candidate in 2000. Though the ticket lost, the Connecticut legislator's religion never became an issue. Many other Jews today also hold political office at all levels.

The Jews of Israel

The sheer numbers of the world's Jews who now live in the United States show that they have found a comfortable fit in American culture. There is, however, a huge difference between the experience of being Jewish in America and in Israel. Though there are almost 6 million Jews in the United States, they constitute only a little over 2 percent of the population. Israel's 4.6 million Jews represent more than 80 percent of its population. This means that in Israel, as in no place else in the world, the vast majority of people walking on the streets, eating in the restaurants, and shopping in the stores are Jewish. It is the only place in the world where Jews are not a minority, where people can assume that they have certain important things in common—a heritage, a destiny, and a shared set of values. It is the only place in the world where festivals like Rosh Hashanah and Passover are national holidays, the only place in the world where Hebrew is the everyday language, and the only place in the world that guarantees a welcome to Jews escaping anti-Semitism elsewhere.

This Jewish identity is a powerful influence in Israel, for it creates a sense of family within the nation. When someone is killed by terrorists in this tiny country, every Israeli feels bereaved. Divisions in Israel run deep, especially between

The Zionists

In 1892 a young journalist named Theodor Herzl stood in a Paris crowd and listened to the chants of "Death to the Jew," as army officer Alfred Dreyfus was stripped of his medals and insignias and sent to prison. Dreyfus had been convicted of treason by a military court, even though evidence pointed to another man, because in the army culture of that era, the unpleasant duty to prosecute a fellow officer could be made less so by targeting a Jew.

Herzl, whose family had left Hungary to escape the pogroms, realized then that there was no safe haven for Jews anywhere. From that moment on, he had a singular focus on the idea of creating a homeland for Jews. Though not the first to have the idea, Herzl's tireless production of books and articles soon led to the first international meeting of a group calling themselves Zionists, after Mount Zion in Jerusalem. Money was raised to buy land in Palestine and send Jewish settlers there to drain swamps, irrigate deserts, plant crops, and build communities. The early settlers, primarily poor eastern Europeans rather than the more comfortable middle-class Jews of western Europe and the United States, suffered from malaria, hunger, and attacks by the local Arab population whose lives were disrupted and communities displaced by these efforts.

Nevertheless the Jews persisted. In 1948 the United Nations formally divided Palestine into Jewish and Arab areas and the independent nation of Israel was declared. The efforts of the Zionists, both in Israel and around the world, had brought to life what had only been prayed for and dreamed about for two thousand years—the return of the children of Israel to their promised land. Today a wooded hill in Jerusalem, home to the burial place of Israel's leaders and fallen soldiers, is named Mount Herzl in Theodor Herzl's honor.

Orthodox Jews and secular, or nonobservant Jews, who are often openly critical of each other for being either too devout or not devout enough. But despite this and other divisions, Israelis know they live in the only place in the world where being a Jew is simply a nonissue.

Visitors to Israel are often surprised by the fact that the country does not seem very religiously observant at all. Nearly three-quarters of Israeli Jews identify themselves as "nonreligious," meaning they do not attend services or make efforts to conform to dietary or other Jewish laws. This is perhaps the ultimate irony, an answer to the Napoleonic era's pronouncements that the Jews were not a people, simply a religion. In Israel today many might argue that the opposite is largely true, that the Jews are very definitely and clearly a people, but no longer united by Judaism.

The Jews of the United States and elsewhere face quite a different situation than those in Israel. They must make deliberate efforts to come together if they are to be part of a Jewish community, and thus places of worship have become the hubs of Jewish life. This is of course not a need for Israeli Jews, for whom even the local mall is a hub of Jewish life. Perhaps the ultimate victory of a Diaspora begun millenia ago is that each part of the Jewish world willingly holds a key to the survival of the rest. An Israeli population largely indifferent to the practice of Judaism protects the promised land for all Jews with their hearts, souls, and lives. American Jews and others around the world join Jewish organizations and participate, often passionately, in efforts to support the Israelis and preserve the home of the heritage they all share.

chapter | four

Jewish Philosophy and Beliefs

A story told about Rabbi Hillel, who lived in the first century A.D., concerns a man who said he would be willing to convert if Hillel could teach him the whole Torah in the amount of time he could stand on one foot. Hillel, one of the greatest and most revered rabbis of all time, is reputed to have said, "That which is hateful to you, do not do unto your neighbor. The rest is commentary. Now go and study."[27] This story has become famous because it captures not only the essential ethic at the core of Judaism, but also the means by which one is to understand that ethic. People are to act justly toward each other, and the way to comprehend what that means is study of the Torah.

Some scholars assert that after the destruction of the Temple by the Romans in A.D. 70, Judaism was a religion without priests. Rabbi Stephen M. Wylen presents quite the opposite view. Jews chose to continue, he writes, "as if they were all priests, and they could recognize God's holy presence anywhere in the world."[28] Activities of the Pharisees around the beginning of the Christian era, including study and personal observance of the Torah, could be practiced by all Jews. All Jews not only could but were required to learn for themselves the mitzvot of the Torah, and then to follow them. All Jewish philosophy from that point

A group of rabbis disputes a point. The Torah has generated centuries of debate, and has shaped the tenets of modern Judaism.

forward has been based on this idea. From it has sprung whole libraries full of the thoughts of brilliant and devout scholars, who over the centuries developed a tradition of lively debate over the underlying meaning of the Torah that has, more than any other single thing, shaped modern Judaism.

But because the purpose of the debate has always been to figure out how to remain true to the covenant while living in a world that does not remotely resemble that of Moses at Sinai, the debate over the meaning of the Torah has been at times heated, at times acrimonious, and often irresolvable. Judaism today shows the marks of many fundamental divisions in thinking among Jews. In fact it is difficult to identify any point on which all Jews agree, except perhaps the thought reflected in the first line of the famous prayer the Shema—there is only one God— and even about that Jewish atheists would beg to differ.

The Oral Torah

Jewish tradition holds that God spoke directly to the Hebrew people at Sinai, giving them the Ten Commandments, and then God conveyed privately to Moses not only the other 603 commandments that are outlined elsewhere in the Torah, but also ritual requirements and practices that were to be passed down orally from generation to generation. In this way Jews would be encouraged to take seriously their personal obligation to preserve the faith. This passing down of traditions from fathers to sons and mothers to daughters became known as the Oral Torah. The concept of the Oral Torah expanded over time to include the teaching of the Sages, as the great rabbis of the early centuries A.D. were known. One major role of the Sages and other rabbinic scholars was to draw inferences from the Torah about how to handle new situations not specifically mentioned therein. These inferences were no less sacred and valid because they were seen not as changing or even adding to the Torah, but as simply enriching understanding of what was always there. In this way, though God no longer spoke directly to human beings, scholars could continue to discern His will through their studies.

Thus from the beginning of Jewish scholarship, the thoughts and words of the rabbis were taken very seriously. Distinguished rabbis such as Hillel and his rival Shammai had large followings in the first century A.D., and from that time forward there were various schools of thought about how to interpret and apply the Torah in daily life. Rabbis studied sacred texts to acquire legal as well as spiritual authority, and the rabbi's status in Jewish society was closely tied to his reputation as a scholar.

The Mishnah

Clearly the massive quantity of scholarly writing generated by the Sages required some method of organization. In the second century A.D., Rabbi Judah ha-Nasi undertook the task of organizing the laws of the Torah and Oral Torah, known as Halakah, as well as a second set of materials called Aggadah, which included Jewish folklore, customs, history, medicine, and astronomy. His work is called the Mishnah. The Mishnah was organized around six basic Sedarim, or Orders: agriculture, observance of Shabbat and holy days, women and the family, legal procedures, dietary laws, and means of ritual purification. The Mishnah was a huge step forward in that it enabled systematic study of Jewish law and custom by future generations of rabbis.

The Mishnah also included important rabbis' commentaries on the Torah. The Mishnah in turn became the subject of extensive commentaries by later rabbis, whose views were dutifully recorded in subsequent editions. The Mishnah was a major text in the curriculum of the yeshiva, as academies of religious study were known. Jewish philosophy continued to evolve as these commentaries proliferated, until once again a new method of organization was needed. Attempts to incorporate the thinking of a growing number of rabbis into the Mishnah were undertaken in Palestine and Babylonia in the fifth and sixth centuries A.D., eventually resulting in the work known as the Talmud.

The Talmud

In Judaism the Talmud is second only to the Bible in its importance as a text. It is organized in the same way as the Mishnah but as Adin Steinsaltz writes in *The Essential Talmud*, it contains "a summarized sketch of the debate of the sages"[29]

The Talmud contains centuries of scholarly debate on ideas of importance in the Jewish faith.

across many generations and in different places, as if they were all in the room arguing at the same time. Traditionally a Talmud page is constructed with only a few lines of the original Mishnah in the center, framed by the rabbis' commentaries, which often take up far more space than the original text. In this way, over the course of years, the Mishnah was studied and discussed piece by piece, and the deliberations recorded in time-honored visual arrangements.

Because Jewish scholars have always valued the insights that sometimes come from associations between ideas that on the surface do not seem very closely related, the editors of the Talmud were not overly concerned with leaps between one subject and another, making the work extremely complex and difficult to follow. A discussion of the use of the story of Esther in the celebration of the spring holiday of Purim, for example, veers off into not only a discussion of the rights of women but also the requirement of a minyan (ten people) for community prayer. Also in keeping with the spirit of debate in Judaism, disagreements between rabbis have been carefully and respectfully recorded, with the understanding that the human

mind can err, the Oral Torah can be misunderstood, and a subject might need to be reexamined later. An expression in the Talmud, "*These* and *these* are *both* the word of the living God,"[30] reflects a sense that some apparent contradictions must simply be accepted as beyond human comprehension but not beyond God's.

The Talmud is full of references to waiting "until Elijah comes" to resolve certain matters. This is a way of saying that some things will become clear only with the level of human understanding that will come in the Messianic Era, an event that will begin with the return of the Prophet Elijah, who died in the ninth century B.C. The complexity and ambiguity of the Talmud has made it an object of lifelong study for rabbis, scholars, and many others to the present today. Its methods are admired not because of their ease but because they are a reflection of a living and evolving faith, created by sincere and passionate efforts to understand the relationship of human beings to God.

The Talmud, even after its widespread dissemination in Jewish communities around the world, was not considered a fixed text in the way that the Torah was. In

The Creation of the Talmud

The Talmud was a huge undertaking by the most renowned Jewish thinkers of the fourth to sixth centuries A.D. But the Talmud could not have been written were it not for the academies that had sprung up around these great rabbis in both Babylonia and Roman Palestine. Of the two, the more significant and lasting contribution was made in Babylonia. In both places, a panel of the most senior and revered rabbis would periodically convene to expound upon something in the Mishnah. All renowned rabbis in the region were in the audience whenever possible, with the pecking order carefully preserved by their assigned seats. Those sitting near the front often asked questions or offered comments and alternative points of view. An audience of local people, including some women, came both for the entertainment value and the potential for spiritual insight provided by the discussion among great minds.

Once disagreements were ironed out, or there was consensus that several views had to be preserved, a commentary summarizing the discussion was prepared. Over years, piece by piece, through the painstaking work of many scholarly editors, the Talmud came into being as the record of these sessions along with supplemental commentaries on the issues. The magnitude of this undertaking is reflected in the fact that all the volumes of a complete Talmud fill a bookshelf three feet long.

A reader uses a pointer to keep his place in the Talmud.

medieval times more commentaries were added, most notably those of the rabbi Shlomo Yitzhaqi, known as Rashi (1040–1105), which now appear as commentaries alongside the original text. Rashi's goal was to provide background information and other clarification that would enable those without a great deal of scholarly background to understand the issues addressed in the Talmud. Others later commented on Rashi, and some of their remarks, called Tosafot, are also included in the Talmud. Even today there is a sense that the Talmud continues to evolve as people study and discuss it, from university scholars to reading groups in local synagogues.

Within this tradition of commentaries upon commentaries it became clear that philosophy was being greatly enriched at the cost of clarity to the typical Jew, who simply wanted to know whether a particular food could be eaten, when to say particular prayers and blessings, how to bury the dead, and other such matters. The great medieval scholar Moses Maimonides (1135–1204), or Moses ben Maimon, generally referred to as the Rambam, was the first to attempt to organize Jewish law in a more accessible manner, but it was not until the sixteenth century that the problem was fully resolved when a rabbi named Joseph Karo created a systematic law code later named the Shulkhan Arukh, Hebrew for "the well-prepared table." Published in 1556, the Shulkhan Arukh was divided into four parts including laws about prayer and ritual, dietary laws, laws involving family and marriage, and civil law. It makes concise and clear statements about what Jewish law is, and for almost five hundred years it has remained the basic authority on the subject.

Divisions Within Unity

Though, in the words of Leo Trepp, Joseph Karo succeeded in writing a work that became "a means of unifying world Jewry,"[31] no one way of being Jewish could possibly have succeeded for the entire population. In fact, from the time of Moses there were categories of Israelites. Jews are classified even today as Kohanim (descendants of the Temple priests), Levites (descendants of those in service to the Temple), or simply Yisrael. Approximately two hundred of the hundreds of mitzvot given to Moses concerned duties of the Kohain (the singular form of Kohanim) and Levite, so when the Temple was destroyed and the priesthood along with it, there was no way to observe these mitzvot. Thus, the custom arose of continuing to distinguish the Kohanim and Levites in certain symbolic and ceremonial ways, to serve as a reminder of the roots of the faith. These distinctions are still observed among traditional Jews. Kohanim, for example, have more restrictions on whom they can marry, and both groups are given certain honors during worship services. Beyond that, today there is little meaning to one's group designation.

The second way Jews have distinguished among themselves is by ethnic branches, which had their beginnings as far back as the destruction of the First Temple. The Ashkenazic Jews are those who settled in eastern and western Europe. The Sephardic Jews are those who settled in the Middle East and North Africa. A third category, Edot ha-Misrach (the Eastern Community) is a blanket term to cover the rest. These distinctions are less pronounced than they once were, because today most of the world's Jews live either in Israel or in the United States, and Sephardic and Ashkenazic Jews attend the same synagogues for the most part, socialize together, and intermarry. The distinctions today are more than anything else a source of pride in the diversity of Jewish culture and evidence of its survival around the world.

The most significant division among Jews today is between Orthodoxy and other forms of Judaism.

Reform rabbi Allan Smith speaks with two Orthodox Jews. Divisions between various sects of the Jewish faith have lessened over the years.

Until the nineteenth century, all Jews believed in the Torah as "eternal, unchangeable, and the sole guide for everyday life and behavior."[32] With the rise of the Reform movement, traditional views were newly labeled "orthodox" to contrast them with "reformed" concepts. The essential difference between Orthodox and Reform Jews is in their view of the Torah. Reform Jews believe that the Torah is the work of divinely inspired people rather than the directly recorded word of God, and consequently they view the Torah as "instructional and inspirational, but not binding, except for the ethical laws."[33] Thus, for Reform Jews, observance of kosher laws and prayer regimens are a matter of informed choice. In other words, being a Reform Jew does not make it acceptable to be ignorant about such things as Jewish ritual blessings and prayers, though a Reform Jew may ultimately choose a different way of expressing a spiritual connection with God. The Orthodox believe in adhering closely to traditional faith and practices, claiming that Jews cannot pick and choose what they like about the covenant and discard the rest. Reform Jews believe that the covenant at Sinai continues to evolve

as the world changes, and the best way to honor it is to live within its framework as a participant in the larger society, reinterpreting Jewish practices as necessary.

Reform Judaism, to many Jews, went too far in its first few generations. Many Reform congregations eliminated almost all the Hebrew from services, for example, and made other changes intended to emphasize similarities to Christianity rather than differences. Many of these changes, such as switching the Sabbath to Sunday, were too extreme and did not last, but for a period of time Jews had only two choices—Orthodoxy or Reform. A third major division in Judaism today, the Conservative movement, was a late nineteenth-century reaction to both. It emphasized both tradition and change, arguing that a living religion must change as the world changes, but that modifications must be introduced for reasons other than mere preference, fashion, or convenience. Modernizing was good only if it was done in a way that recognized the binding nature of Jewish law and preserved traditions important to retaining a distinct Jewish identity. Conservative Judaism reintroduced many rituals, emphasized the use of Hebrew in

Holy Sparks

Medieval Jewish philosophers known as mystics believed that the Torah was more than just a text of history and laws, and that God had used the letters and numbers in it to encode hidden meanings about the design of the universe. Through it they believed they could find "insights into the nature of God, the creation of the Universe, the destiny of human beings, the nature of evil, and the ultimate meaning of Torah," as Leo Trepp explains in *A History of the Jewish Experience.*

The term "Kabbalah" ("receiving tradition") is used to identify Jewish mystical ideas in general. At its core are the ten *sefirot* (emanations or channels) elucidated in the thirteenth-century Spanish text, the *Zohar,* and expounded upon by other mystics such as Isaac Luria (1534–1572), also known as Ari. Taken together the ten *sefirot* are the means by which God ordered His universe, and in balance they bring about a just and merciful world. This system is so complicated that it can be studied for a lifetime, and often is, but for most Jews, the details of the *sefirot* are not as important as the message they send about human responsibility for contributing to the restoration of order in a world negatively impacted by human shortcomings. The key to setting the world right is observance of the mitzvot. Today the rigid adherence of many Orthodox Jews to the minute details of Jewish law stems from this idea, which is likened to the collecting of holy sparks and bringing them back to their source, God. As George Robinson explains in *Essential Judaism: A Complete Guide to Beliefs, Customs, and Rituals,* "every time that a human performs a mitzvah, she raises one of the holy sparks out of the hands of the forces of evil . . . and every time that a human sins, a divine spark plunges down."

Jewish mysticism has two important strands. One is the intense study of the Torah for clues as to God's meaning, plan, and will. The other is the experience of union with God through a form of altered consciousness entered by intently focused prayer and meditation, which sometimes takes the form of dancing, swaying, chanting, or other forms of expression. One strand is intellectual and can be practiced only by those well versed in sacred texts, but the other can be embraced by anyone who wishes to participate. Both forms of mysticism are becoming increasingly popular today.

services, reaffirmed the importance of all the mitzvot, and serves today as another alternative to Orthodox and Reform Judaism.

What Jews Believe

A long history of valuing debate, as reflected in the Talmud and other texts, as well as simple disagreements today, make it difficult to pin down exactly what all Jews believe, although there are a few binding precepts that are clearly shared by most, or at least acknowledged as central to Judaism. The cornerstone of the Jewish faith is that there is only one God and that God is king of the whole universe. Jewish doctrine holds that because Moses and his followers accepted His commandments at Mount Sinai a special relationship exists between God and all Jews that obligates them to a high standard of behavior. Jews are taught that a truly fulfilling life comes from loving and serving God. This includes stopping to praise and to bless the name of God for things that might otherwise go unnoticed, such as bread on the table, or the act of awakening in the morning, or bringing light into a dark room. It also includes caring for the less fortunate, being honest in all dealings, and in raising children to love God and be good neighbors.

Most Jews believe, as a logical consequence of all this, that life is precious and it should be lived to the fullest, and many feel that this can be done only within the context of sacred law. For example, they would argue that God gave people taste buds with which to enjoy what they eat; therefore, it cannot be contrary to God's will to take pleasure in food. Thus, denying oneself adequate and flavorful food is not a way to show gratitude or devotion. However, many Jews believe that from time to time fasting is a good way of acknowledging God's power in providing the special gift of pleasure in food, and to remind people to reflect on how they are handling the greatest gift of all, the opportunity to be alive. Also, though most Jews who keep kosher dietary laws do so simply because "God said so," they come to understand that this dietary discipline encourages reflection both on how God plays a role in sustaining their life through the bounty of the land and on the sacrifice of life required to put food on their table.

What Jews Do Not Believe

Jews, on the other hand, reject certain ideas of other faiths, particularly some key concepts in Christianity. In the words of nineteenth-century philosopher Moses Mendelssohn, "There is not one single commandment in Mosaic law telling us 'Thou shalt believe' or 'not believe.' Faith is not commanded. In questions of eternal truth nothing is said of believing, the terms are understanding and knowing."[34] This emphasis on acceptance of the "eternal truth" of God's existence and absolute authority is in contrast to the Christian concept of a God whose existence one experiences personally, or at least hopes to, in some manner or form. To Jews, as Mendelssohn explains, personal realization or acceptance has little to do with the matter. God simply is, and Jews strive to know and understand this. One does not need, as a show of faith, deliberately to put one's life in God's hands, for it already is and always has been there.

Jews also do not share the central tenet of Christianity, that the messiah came to earth in the form of Jesus of Nazareth. They are certain Jesus could not have been the messiah because he did not fulfill the prophecy of ushering in the perfect and harmonious world of the promised Messianic Age. They also take issue with the Christian concept of salvation through faith.

To Jews, forgiveness can only be granted by the person one has wronged, after which one can ask forgiveness of God, but the idea that the actions of one individual can serve to atone for the sins of another, as Jesus is said to have done for all who believe in him, is not part of Judaism.

Additionally, the concept of original sin, the idea that humans are born in a state of sin from which only faith can redeem them, is not in keeping with Jewish thinking. Jews believe humans are born with a clean slate, and once they can distinguish right from wrong, they are free to choose between the two. Consequences that come from their choices are earned and are their responsibility alone. Free will is an essential aspect of human life. Related to this is the Jewish belief that evil exists because people are free to choose it. To Jews it is erroneous to attribute bad choices and bad events to an evil power such as the Devil. It is simply to be expected that the human race will do the whole range of things of which it is capable, including unspeakably vile acts. God has made clear what He expects, and the rest is up to the individual.

What Jews do or do not believe about the afterlife is more compli-

A Star of David adorns a grave stone. The idea of eternal punishmnet is not a part of Judaism's view of death.

cated. One Jew may believe that death is simply the end of existence, whereas another may believe there is some sort of afterlife of the soul, but the elaborate descriptions of heaven and hell common to Christianity are not part of Jewish thinking. Many Jews believe in some sort of judgment day, but one of the few things about which there is general agreement is that there is no such thing as eternal punishment. What is far more important to Jews is the way their lives on Earth are handled. As George Robinson explains, "the one certain form of life after death is the deeds we do while we are here."[35] The consequences of what people do, and the way they are remembered, Jews view as a form of immortality. Furthermore, many Jews think concentrating on the afterlife is an error. Jews should behave properly simply because God has commanded it, not in hope of some big reward later. The reward is received in this life, in the form of the contentment and peace that comes from keeping the covenant.

Finally, Jews do not believe that their being "chosen" means that they should feel superior to other people. It simply means that God expects each of them to serve as an example of an ethical life. Some Jews, followers of the Jewish mystical tradition known as Kabbalah, believe that every time they observe a mitzvah, they pick up a divine spark and return it to God. Some say the messiah will come when all Jews follow all the mitzvot given by God at Mount Sinai. Other Jews may not share either of these visions, but nevertheless, one of the basic precepts of Judaism, *tikkun olam,* or "repairing the world," shows how deeply ingrained the idea of contributing to the betterment of the world is in Jewish thinking. Regardless of whether one is Ashkenazic or Sephardic, Orthodox or Reform, Kohain or Levite, perhaps the most binding view among Jews is that all people have the power—and Jews have the obligation—to live their lives in a way that honors all of God's creation, and thus makes life on Earth a little better.

chapter | five

Living a Jewish Life

Some say there are as many different ways to be Jewish as there are Jews. This was not always the case. In the past, despite cultural differences, Jews in a shtetl in the Pale, the deserts of Morocco, and the neighborhoods of Paris were linked by a clear code of binding Jewish law. Therefore, how they expressed their Jewishness might be different in the details, but at its core it consisted of the same Hebrew prayers, the same restrictions on diet, the same rituals. This began to change with the splintering of Judaism into Orthodox, Reform, Conservative, and more recently into Reconstructionist, Jewish Renewal, and other approaches to the faith. Nevertheless, with the exception of those Jews who see being Jewish as simply a matter of heredity and do not acknowledge any aspect of the faith as relevant to their lives, the vast majority would agree that certain activities are central to Jews.

Shabbat

Most central of all is Shabbat, the Sabbath. It, like all Jewish days, is measured from sundown Friday to sundown Saturday. As traditionally observed, Shabbat is a time when no work is done. Instead, the day is turned over to those activities that renew the spirit. It is a time of good food, the company of family and friends, and of

What Is Work?

The Sabbath is the only day important enough to be mentioned in the Ten Commandments. Jews have interpreted the commandment to "remember the Sabbath and keep it holy" to mean that people should rest, as God did after the creation. But rest, or *menucha* in Hebrew, does not mean spending the day frivolously. Rather, it is a suspension for one day a week of the routines of school and work, in an attempt to feel a greater sense of holiness in the world and in one's own life.

To accomplish this, the Talmud established thirty-nine categories of work that should be avoided on Shabbat or Shabbos, the two names by which the Jews refer to the Sabbath. These fall under general categories relevant to an earlier age—agricultural work, work with cloth or leather, writing, construction work, and activities involving fire. Examples of forbidden activities include picking fruit or cutting flowers, sewing on a button, writing, or even cutting something out of the newspaper. After the candles are lit on Friday night and Shabbat officially begins, prohibitions against fire include striking a match or otherwise starting or transferring a flame. Thus, smoking is prohibited, as is lighting a burner to cook food. Because eating is a big part of the Shabbat celebration, all cooking and activity involving "separating the useful from the useless," (one of the Talmudic categories) such as pitting fruit or peeling carrots, must be done before sundown on Friday.

Acts that change the natural environment in any way, however small, are work. Likewise, any physical act that has lasting value is work. Many Jews follow Shabbat prohibitions very strictly, but the typical Jew is likely to pick and choose, or perhaps follow none of the restrictions at all. To observant Jews, however, limiting the things one can do on Shabbat is a pleasure, because it provides a psychological break from the rest of the week—a true sense of rest.

Havdalah candles (pictured) are used to mark the end of the Sabbath.

course, the worship of God. At sundown the lighting of candles and a series of blessings welcome Shabbat. A Sabbath dinner is leisurely eaten at a table that has been set with special care. Services are held at the temple early Friday evening as well as Saturday morning, and many Jews try to attend one or the other. Because, for observant Jews, Shabbat is a different kind of day in which regular activities are not done, Saturday services have an unrushed feeling. They last several hours and often include rituals associated with life passages, such as the celebration of weddings, baby namings, and the like.

After services, Shabbat continues with another meal, followed by family activities, quiet study, or perhaps even a nap. A little after sundown, calculated in earlier times as the moment at which three stars could be seen in the evening sky, a closing ceremony known as Havdalah is held. A special braided candle is lit; another series of blessings, prayers, and rituals are performed; then the candle is extinguished and everyone wishes each other a good week.

Daily Prayer and Its Rituals

Shabbat begins and ends with prayers and special blessings, as does

A Jewish family combines the Shabbat meal with the Passover Seder. This happens when Passover falls on Shabbat.

every other aspect of an observant Jewish life. From childhood, Jews are exposed to the idea that "there is almost no aspect of life for which an observant Jew does not thank and bless the Creator."[36] Thus during the course of a day, many Jews will offer blessings over the foods and beverages they eat, as well as special blessings for privileges such as experiencing something of exceptional beauty or fragrance, or on receiving good or bad news. An observant Jew's daily routine begins by thanking God for restoring his or her soul in the morning with the reciting of Modeh Ani, followed by a ritual washing of hands. A man worshiping at home may put on a prayer shawl and tefillin, also known as phylacteries. These are small boxes containing words from the Shema, which are secured on the forehead and the inner forearm, fulfilling the commandment to keep the word of God between one's eyes and to bind it upon one's arm. He will then recite the morning service from the siddur, or prayer book, with *kavanah*, or intention not just to finish it but truly to communicate with God.

If he goes to the synagogue or other prayer center he will "daven" there, a term meaning to be "deeply, emotionally involved" in prayer,

"caught up in the immediate reality of speaking to God, of knowing God is listening and of hearing God in return."[37] Community prayer requires a minyan, a group of no fewer than ten worshippers, to go forward with certain aspects of the service, including the Mourner's Kaddish, one version of the important basic prayer known as the kaddish. The Mourner's Kaddish is required daily of observant Jews for up to eleven months when an immediate family member dies, and therefore some Jews not in mourning themselves make a point of going to daily services, to ensure that mourners will be able to recite this prayer.

Prayers are also offered in the afternoon and the evening seven days a week, either at the synagogue or at home, following much the same basic structure as the morning service, but with some changes based on tradition or Jewish law. Several prayers have central roles in all services, and in fact, Jews see the rest of the service as leading in and out of these central components. The two most important prayers are the Shema and the *Amidah*, which along with the kaddish (a statement of praise of God) and the *Aleinu* (a proclamation of God as absolute ruler) provide a structure

Hebrew School

One of the main obligations of Jewish parents is to see to the proper education of their children. Increasing numbers of Jewish parents are sending their children to private Jewish elementary and high schools, but this is not always possible. However, the long-standing tradition of Hebrew school is a means by which all Jewish children can become knowledgeable of their heritage. Hebrew school evolved as an after-school or Sunday program primarily but not exclusively for children who attend regular schools during the day and thus are not exposed to religious material. In Hebrew school, young Jews practice reading and writing Hebrew, study the Bible, and learn about Jewish history. They also celebrate Jewish holidays and take field trips to events featuring Jewish artists or themes. Many Hebrew schools also expose older children to issues affecting them as members of the global Jewish community, such as terrorism in Israel.

for worship. As George Robinson points out, "In a religion noticeably devoid of statements of creed, [the Shema] is as close as you can come to a statement of faith."[38] It announces the oneness of God and commands Jews to remember God day in and day out, and to pass their faith on to their children. It stresses that the people of Israel will succeed or fail based on how well they keep God's commandments. The *Amidah* is a series of anywhere from seven to nineteen blessings of praise, supplication, and thanksgiving, depending on the particular service. It serves in miniature as a statement of Jewish concepts about God and His relationship to His creation.

Living Halakically

There is more, however, to being a Jew than regular prayer. In fact, Jews would say that is only the beginning. Judaism is based around family and the larger community. The concept of a minyan, for example, is designed to remind Jews not to focus only on their own personal connection to God, but to enhance that connection by contact with others. Jews know that the commandments are designed to guide people to live in harmony with each other and with the environment, for only in that manner can God truly be pleased.

The term "halakah" refers to Jewish law, and when a person lives in accordance with that law, he or she

Kashruth

One of the hallmarks of living an observant Jewish life is following the Jewish dietary laws of kashruth, commonly referred to as "keeping kosher." There are only a few fundamental components to this. The first is that meat and dairy products can never be mixed, even in separate dishes, at the same meal. The second is that certain foods, most notably pork and anything from the ocean (or other body of water) that does not have both fins and scales, cannot be eaten at all. A third is that animals must be slaughtered in a way that minimizes suffering and which drains the carcass of blood, which was considered by the ancient Hebrews to be the life spirit of the animal. Kosher laws also extend to the preparation of food. The same cutting boards, knives and other utensils, pans, dishes, and silverware are not used to prepare both meat and dairy foods, nor are items used for dairy washed together with those for meat.

The basis for kashruth is a number of commandments in the Torah in which God simply states what can and cannot be eaten. As a result, a variety of kosher cooking styles evolved using local ingredients wherever Jews lived. Sephardic cooking emphasizes the grains, legumes, vegetables, and spices prevalent in the Middle East and North Africa, whereas Ashkenazi cooking favors the starches and meats of eastern Europe. In the last century, many Jews decided that the rules of kashruth were no longer a necessary part of the practice of Judaism, but by that point the traditional kosher recipes associated with the Jewish table had already evolved.

Today much is made of the fact that the prohibitions make excellent sense health-wise, and some suggest that the commandments are better seen as reflecting the folk wisdom of the Hebrews than the will of God. However, many Jews bristle at the suggestion that keeping kosher is meant to be practical. It is a mitzvah, or special duty, and offering any other justification seems to imply that serving God is not a sufficient one. To observant Jews, the family table is a kind of altar, a place where the blessings of life can be most fully appreciated. Choosing and preparing food carefully helps bring a sense of holiness into family life, and mindfulness of the God who provides it all.

is said to be living halakically. There are several key components to this, in addition to regular prayer. Perhaps the most familiar aspect of halakic life is the dietary law laid out in the Torah, kashruth, commonly referred to as "keeping kosher." Though to many Jews keeping a kosher household is regarded as the "backbone of Jewish life," writer C.M. Pilkington adds that "standards of observance are not particularly high . . . and are continuing to decline."[39] The main reason for this is that most Jews are not willing to turn diet into an issue that sets them apart from their non-Jewish friends and colleagues. Strict kosher observance precludes eating in nonkosher restaurants or nonkosher homes. The majority of Jews see this as carrying halakah to an unnecessary extreme, feeling that dietary laws should be observed "not because they are given by God to Moses, but because they may encourage self-discipline and a sense of Jewish identity."[40]

Tzedaka

One other major element in living halakically is *tzedaka.* Often mistranslated as charity, *tzedaka,* in fact, means justice in Hebrew. The world will not treat all people equally, Jews believe, but all have a right to be sustained by the bounty of the earth. In biblical times, farmers would leave the corners of their fields unharvested so people in need could come and take food to live on, as their right. Jewish *tzedaka* today is a continuation of this concept. Thus, when a Jew puts money in the *tzedaka* box kept in many homes, he or she is not to think of this as a praiseworthy act. It is simply money that is to be donated as a matter of course to an organization serving the needy. The Book of Deuteronomy in the Torah mentions that Jews should give 10 percent of their income as a minimum to charitable institutions. Even Jews who cannot afford that are expected to give something, and though not all Jews do so, the notion of the obligation to make a contribution to justice is a deep-seated Jewish value. Indeed Jews, representing only 2 percent of the world's population, have a reputation for social involvement and giving far beyond their numbers.

Jewish Marriage

In addition to kashruth and *tzedaka,* there are mitzvot, or commandments, covering many other aspects of family and community life. Marriage is seen as the ideal

Guests dance with the bride at a traditional Jewish wedding celebration.

way to go through adult life, and there is significant pressure on single adults to find a partner and start a family. One midrash states that "woman was not created from man's head that she should dominate him, or from his feet, that he should dominate her, but from his side, that they should be equal partners."[41] Until recently, men and women traditionally had specific roles, the woman in the home and the man in the world of work, but these were viewed as equal in the shaping and sustaining of a Jewish family, which was the most important single goal in life. The Bible specifically admonishes men not to cause their wives grief by their behavior, and wives are similarly told not to turn the home into a place of conflict. A substantially lower divorce rate for American Jewish couples may be evidence that these warnings are taken to heart at least by some.

Jewish weddings are very festive events, held under a *huppa*, or canopy, symbolizing the couple's home and their unity under its roof. At the end of the ceremony, the groom smashes a glass under his heel to symbolize the destruction of the Temple, a reminder that even in the midst of happiness there is sorrow. The ceremony is followed by a noisy party celebrating the couple and their future together.

Observing Life Passages

Because Jews are generally small minorities wherever they live, and because they have been subject to attempts at annihilation throughout the past, Judaism places very high value on marriages that produce children. Thus, a birth is treated with great joy. Eight days after birth, a boy child is marked as a Jew with the sign of the covenant and given his Hebrew name in a special ceremony known as a Brith Milah, or bris. The marking involves circumcision, snipping off the foreskin of the penis, sometimes by the father but more often by a *mohel,* a specially trained rabbi. Although concerned about the fleeting pain to the infant, Jews find the bris a deeply moving experience because it symbolizes their continuation as a people more than any other single act. Female infants are entered into to the Jewish community and given their Hebrew names in a ceremony at the synagogue. The newborns will be called by their Hebrew names throughout life at Jewish ceremonies.

The next significant life passage for many Jews is the bar mitzvah for a boy at thirteen or bat mitzvah for a girl when she turns twelve or thirteen. After that point the next important passage is marriage. Even at the bris and baby namings for girls, and the bar and bat mitzvah ceremonies, reference is made to standing under the *huppa* to be married in the years ahead, a clear indication that Jews think of life as a series of passages.

The Jewish Way of Death

The final passage, of course, is death, and Jewish customs and law provide for this in a way that honors the dead, affirms the wonder and beauty of life, and helps the mourners deal with their grief.

When a person nears death, a special society of volunteers called the Chevra Kadisha is often involved in ensuring that the death is as spiritual an experience as possible. Ideally the person dies with the Shema on his or her lips. After death, the Chevra Kadisha or the mortuary performs the duties of preparing the body for burial by ritual cleansing, wrapping in a shroud, putting the tallith, or prayer shawl (with its *tzitzit,* or fringes,

Becoming an Adult

One of the most significant life passages for Jews is the bar mitzvah for a boy at thirteen or bat mitzvah for a girl when she turns twelve or thirteen. To Jews, these are the ages of adulthood in regard to matters of religious observance and responsibility for one's actions. The term bar or bat mitzvah means son or daughter of the commandment and implies a willing acceptance of the mitzvot of the Torah. This event is often celebrated with a formal ceremony at the synagogue followed by a party, but a Jew is considered an adult at this point regardless of whether any ceremony is held.

A bar or bat mitzvah celebration can take a number of different forms, but religious ceremonies center around an aliyah, a calling to read the Torah. Typically, the sacred scrolls are physically handed down through any generations of the family who are present, as a means of symbolizing the passing of knowledge and responsibility. After receiving the Torah in this manner, the bar or bat mitzvah celebrant parades the Torah around the synagogue. He or she recites various blessings and may chant passages from the Torah and haftarah, a biblical text related to the theme of the Torah passage. The reading of the Torah must be done directly from the scrolls, which are in Hebrew and are not marked in any way for the melody or pronunciation of the words. Learning the tropes, or melodies, and how to apply them to the words of the Torah and haftarah is a major undertaking requiring months of study and is considered a mark of the young man or woman's commitment to Judaism.

A Jewish boy celebrating his bar mitzvah carries the Torah in the company of his family.

Cutting the fringes of the tallith (pictured) symbolizes that a deceased Jew has no further obligation to prayer.

cut to show that the dead have no further obligations of prayer) over the shoulders, and laying the body in a plain wooden coffin. Human remains are not embalmed or cremated, nor are more elaborate coffins used unless required by law. This is because the dead are supposed to return to the dust from which they symbolically came as completely and as quickly as possible. For this reason, burial takes

place the same day as death, if possible, or as soon after as can be arranged.

When a person dies, the immediate family enters a phased process of mourning. After the graveside services, the mourners recite the Kaddish prayer for the dead and may make a symbolic tear in their clothing to represent the tear in their lives. Once they return home they begin sitting *shivah,* a seven-day period during which many symbolic acts are performed, such as sitting on low stools or the floor, covering mirrors, and avoiding personal grooming. Family and friends visit, an essential mitzvah (good deed) because the mourners will not leave the house during the whole seven days except on Shabbat to attend services. Thus, others must meet their needs by bringing food, running errands, and making up the minyan for the Mourner's Kaddish.

After the seven days, life must be resumed to a certain degree, but formal mourning for a relative other than a parent continues for thirty days, and for a parent it continues for eleven months. For the rest of their lives, children will observe the anniversary, or *yahrzeit,* of the parent's death by visiting the grave and by making an aliyah, which involves reciting a blessing over the Torah during Shabbat services.

The High Holy Days

Yahrzeits take their place in the annual cycle of Jewish celebrations. This cycle begins with a ten-day period known as the High Holy Days, or the Days of Awe. The holy days begin in September or early October with Rosh Hashanah ("Head of the Year"), observed on the first day of the Jewish month of Tishri, and they end with Yom Kippur, the Day of Atonement, the most solemn day of the Jewish year. The entire period of the High Holy Days is a time of self-assessment, including reflection on one's shortcomings and mistakes in the last year, conscientious attempts to seek forgiveness for them and set them right if possible, atonement before God, and meditation on how to live a better life in the coming year. Rosh Hashanah begins with a festive meal including apples dipped in honey to symbolize wishes for a good year, followed by a synagogue service. On the following morning one of the most moving events in Judaism takes place at the morn-

ing service. There, the shofar, or ram's horn, is blown at several points in the service. Leo Trepp describes the sound as "weird, primitive, produced without concern for key and harmony,"[42] and Wayne Dosick adds that the "heart piercing blast of the shofar" serves as a reminder of "Judaism's beginnings in a long-ago, far-away desert . . . , [the] perfect sound to lead the way toward soul inventory and to direct the path toward God."[43]

A rabbi blows the ram's horn during a Rosh Hashanah service.

The next eight days are a chance for continued reflection on how the individual and the Jewish community as a whole have failed "to apply [God's] divine yardstick"[44] to their lives. Jews are expected to act as if the end of the High Holy Days, symbolically seen as the sealing of the Book of Life, is the last chance they will have in life to set things straight. But the time is not gloomy, for Jews know that true repentance is always met with divine mercy, and that failings properly atoned for will be forgiven. Proper atonement includes, for example, not simply being sorry for having taken something belonging to someone else, but going to that person, confessing, and offering to repay. Only after suitable atonement can God's forgiveness be sought.

The High Holy Days end with Yom Kippur. Yom Kippur begins with a substantial meal before sunset, for after that meal observant Jews will take not even a bite of food or a sip of water for twenty-four hours or more. At sunset the service begins with the Kol Nidre, an ancient prayer that sets the tone of genuine repentance and joy in God's mercy. The following day services are ongoing at the synagogue until sunset. Memorial prayers for one's own dead and for Jewish martyrs and Holocaust victims are said, and the book of Jonah is read in its entirety. At sunset, the Shema is recited and the shofar sounds for the last time. The congregation says "Next year in Jerusalem" to signify the desire for "an end to exile and return to the land of Israel, and at the same time a prayer for ultimate redemption, for peace and perfection for the entire world."[45] Buoyed by the spirit of the ten days, Jews then break the fast by sharing a meal with friends and family.

The Pilgrimage Festivals

Second only to the High Holy Days is Passover, or Pesach, one of three pilgrimage festivals celebrated by the ancient Hebrews. The other two are Shavuoth, a spring harvest celebration, and Sukkoth, a fall harvest celebration. They are called pilgrimage festivals because they are the three times a year that travel to the Temple in Jerusalem was required so that payment in the form of tithes of crops could be made. Passover (Pesach) is the most beloved holy day, and the most universally celebrated by Jews. Passover commemorates the liberation of the Hebrews from slavery in Egypt.

Former Israeli prime minister Benjamin Netanyahu (left) helps his son prepare matzo, the traditional unleavened bread of Passover.

Moses told the Israelites to make a mark on their doors so that an angel sent from God to kill all the firstborn of Egypt would pass over their homes and spare them. When the pharaoh's firstborn son was killed, he was so agonized by this loss that he agreed to let the Hebrews go free.

To commemorate this event, several very special activities are incorporated into Passover. First, because the Hebrews left in such a hurry that they could not let their bread rise before baking, Jews eat no soft, or leavened, bread for eight days. Instead they eat a baked cracker, called matzo, to commemorate the sun-baked flour that sustained their ancestors on their flight. In observant homes, great care is taken to remove even crumbs of leavened bread from the home. The first evening of Pesach is the most festive night of the Jewish year, when the meal known as the Seder is celebrated. During the celebration, the story of the escape from Egypt is told and symbolic foods are eaten to reinforce the message of the story. A special text known as the Passover Haggadah is

Party Time

Some Jewish holidays are solemn events, and some mix seriousness with gaiety, but two have evolved into holidays primarily associated with fun. The first, Hanukkah, has gained in emphasis in recent years as a way to provide a celebration for Jewish children while others are celebrating Christmas. Hanukkah, which commemorates Judah Maccabee's victory over the Greek tyrant Antiochus, is also called the Festival of Lights because it centers on the story of the miraculous burning of a Temple lamp for eight days with an oil supply that should only have lasted one. A special nine-branched menorah called a *Hanukia* is used to hold candles, and a special center candle, the shammes, or "servant," is used to light them, one additional candle each day. Children often receive a small gift each day, and Hanukkah parties abound, featuring latkes, a traditional potato pancake. One traditional game is played with a top known as a dreidel, which has Hebrew letters on its side. Players put coins or candies in the pot, and then take turns spinning the dreidel to see whether they get to take something out of the pot or put something more in.

Purim is a spring celebration commemorating the biblical heroine Esther, who manages to get her husband, the king of Persia, to spare the lives of the Jews and put to death the villain, Haman, who had plotted to destroy them. Purim is a time for costumes and parties that include loud shouting to drown out the name of Haman when the story is told. Traditional fruit-filled cookies named hamantaschen (Haman's pockets) are a special Purim treat.

A menorah with nine branches is the symbol of Hanukkah, a Jewish holiday which commemorates the victory of Judah over the Greek tyrant Antiochus.

used, which contains the story of the exodus from Egypt, the blessings that are to be said at the meal, the order of events in the Seder dinner, and the symbolic meaning of the foods and gestures. Bitter herbs and salt water, for example, represent the bitterness and tears of their lives as slaves, and spilled drops of wine represent the plagues that fell on the people of Egypt because of the pharaoh's hard heart. Central to the message of the Seder is that the liberation from slavery and the Hebrews' safe deliverance out of Egypt did not just happen to Jews who lived long ago, but should be treated as something God did to show his eternal and abiding love for each Jew, past, present, and future. Hence the Seder is a show of gratitude to God by all the celebrants for the blessing of freedom in their own lives.

Time to Remember

The Jewish year is replete with other holidays as well. Tishah-b'Ab, for example, is a day of fasting to commemorate the destruction of the Temple. In the twentieth century several other holidays were added to the Jewish calendar to commemorate more recent events.

The first is Yom ha-Shoa, a day of remembrance and mourning for the Jews murdered in the Holocaust. The second is the two-day celebration of Israel's victory in the War of Independence in 1948, which brought it into being as an independent Jewish nation. The day before Yom ha-Atzma'ut (Independence Day) is Yom ha-Zikaron, the day of remembrance of those killed. On this day a siren blares in Israel and a minute of respectful silence is held for all those killed in Israel's wars. Traffic comes to a complete stop, and people stand by their cars with bowed heads. In the United States many synagogues and Jewish community centers also commemorate these holidays.

Though much of Judaism is practiced quietly, from cradle to grave, from one sunset to another, and from one season to the next, the Jewish year provides constant reminders of who the Jews are. They are the beneficiaries of one of the great wisdom traditions of the world. Each Jew is a thread in the continuation of that tradition, living in a God-created and God-centered world in which the privileges and responsibilities of life can never be taken for granted.

chapter | six

New Songs and Ancient Themes: Jewish Arts and Culture

When King David brought the ark bearing the stone tablets of the Ten Commandments into Jerusalem, he ran "leaping and whirling before the Lord,"[46] so unconcerned for his dignity as king that his wife Michal reprimanded him later. The psalms attributed to David are filled with references to making music. Psalm 33, for example, is one of many calling upon the people of Israel to "Praise the Lord with the lyre/with the ten stringed harp sing to Him/Sing Him a new song/Play sweetly with shouts of joy."[47] The ark David danced before was lavishly and lovingly adorned with gold, silver, precious stones, and fine woods. Clearly, expressing feelings about God through the exuberance of music and the finest works of the hands has been a hallmark of Judaism since its beginnings.

The Art of the Synagogue
Synagogues of Europe and the Middle East express well this desire to lavish praise on God through fine works of

art. However, the Ten Commandments forbid creating "graven images," which in Moses's time meant anything carved or molded into a statue. In time, it came to mean any attempt to represent God, which was impossible, or any other image that might become an object of worship. Instead, Jewish artisans perfected techniques to decorate the items used in worship and to beautify their synagogues or temples.

Because in many cultures Jewish worship was severely restricted, synagogues tend to be small and hidden away from public view. Non-Jews might walk down a street for years and have no idea what beauty lies behind the shabby gate through which black-hatted men

Hungarian president Arpad Goencz talks with former Israeli prime minister Yitzak Shamir at Europe's largest synagogue in Budapest, Hungary.

pass several times a day. Once inside, worshipers take their places around the four sides of a central, raised wooden pulpit, or bema. On the bema is a table where the Torah is read. The bema and the table often are beautifully carved or painted, and woven or embroidered banners in a riot of lush colors and fabrics decorate the walls. On one wall, oriented so that someone looking at it would be facing Jerusalem, the Torah is housed in cabinets covered with beautiful curtains. From these cabinets the scrolls of the Torah are taken out during particular services, paraded through the sanctuary for people to see and touch, and then brought to the bema to be read. The ceiling of the synagogue, typically a dome, often is brightly decorated with stars, bird or animal motifs, and other designs. Often the synagogue is lit with sparkling chandeliers, making the overall effect a dance of colors and textures designed to remind the viewer that praising God is something that can be done at all times in many different ways.

Many of these old synagogues have been destroyed over the years, often deliberately in anti-Semitic attacks, or indirectly by civil ordinances forbidding maintenance work so the buildings would collapse from neglect. Modern synagogues frequently are designed differently, more like churches, with rows of seats facing a raised platform from which the service is conducted. Nevertheless, many other features provide continuity with the past, such as decorated arks in front of which burns the *ner tamid*, or "eternal light"; embroidered velvet or silk Torah covers (or gold or silver cases in Sephardic congregations); and pointers, often in filigreed silver, used to facilitate reading the scrolls.

Prayer Objects

The decorative impulse in Judaism is also expressed through objects used in prayer. Most notable among these is the tallith, or prayer shawl. Traditionally, prayer shawls are white with black or blue stripes, although in recent times textile designers have begun making colorful and luxurious variations. What distinguishes a prayer shawl are the fringes at the corners. Each tassel, or *tzitzit*, is made of knotted threads to represent the number 613, the number of commandments. The symbolic importance of the *tzitzit* comes from the idea of wrapping oneself up in the commandments as a way of life, and in fact the only ritually important part of the prayer shawl is the *tzitzit*. In biblical times the fringes were directly attached to clothing and worn all day, a practice continued today by some Orthodox men, who wear a special undergarment with a *tzitzit* attached to each corner.

Another item worn by Orthodox and many Conservative Jewish men are tefillin, or phylacteries, little boxes containing the words from the Torah that command the words of God be bound upon the hand and between the eyes. These are strapped in a symbolic and ritualistic way around the head, hand, and forearm as a means of becoming focused on worship. According to Rabbi Wayne Dosick, "the ritual remains one of Jewish identity, Jewish commitment, and a visible, dramatic connection to God and His commandments."[48]

A third item of apparel not directly connected to acts of prayer but that has a similar "visible, dramatic connection" is the *kippah*, known in Yiddish as a yarmulke. This is the round skullcap worn by Orthodox Jews throughout the day, and by Conservative and some Reform Jews during worship, study, and eating. The idea of the *kippah* is to show respect for God by keeping one's head covered.

Kippot are often plain black, but they can also be knit or embroidered with colorful accents.

Candles and Kiddush Cups: Art in the Jewish Home

In addition to synagogue art and objects used personally, several important items used in the home traditionally have been the subject of great decorative traditions. The seven-branched candlestick known as a menorah (and its nine-branched variant used for Hanukkah) are fixtures in most Jewish homes. Because the family table is seen as a kind of altar, much of the Jewish love of decoration has gone into items used for meals and home celebrations. The kiddush cup, used for the ritual blessing over wine, and a minimum of two candlesticks are standard features of the Shabbat table. Some Shabbat tables are also set with embroidered covers for the two loaves of challah, or braided bread, that is traditional for Shabbat, as well as a spice box used for the Havdalah ceremony that ends Shabbat with a lingering pleasant smell. Holidays have their own traditional objects as well, such as the Seder plate for the symbolic foods of Passover. Contemporary artists have turned to these ritual objects and

A Jewish table boasts Shabbat candles, matzo, traditional Jewish table wine, and challah bread.

created art pieces for the table in a wide variety of styles, from angular, contemporary candlesticks, to hand-painted porcelain plates, to rustic pottery kiddush cups, to hand-painted silk challah covers, to more traditional renditions.

Several other objects not associated with the table also characterize Jewish homes. The most important is the mezuzah. This is a small container affixed to the door frame of a Jewish home, in keeping with the commandment to keep the words of God on the doorposts and gates of dwellings. Some people hang them on the doors of each major room in the house except the bathroom, but minimally a Jewish home will have one at the front entrance to the home. The important aspect of the mezuzah is the tiny parchment inside it on which the relevant words are written, but over the years the casing around the scroll has become an outlet for artistic expression. Today mezuzot can be found in a wide

Creating a Torah

Creating a new Torah is painstaking and very time consuming. The whole process takes more than a year and is considered one of the greatest mitzvot in Judaism. Rabbi Shmuel Miller describes in "Inspiration and Craft: Becoming a Scribe," how a North African sofer, *or Torah maker, named Ribbi Haim, completes the process.*

"When a Sefer Torah is ordered, Ribbi Haim . . . first soaks the hides of a hundred sheep in a large pond of water for three consecutive days. The water is [brought] from the well to the pond by a camel. For another ten days the skins are soaked in [lime water], which allows the wool and the meat left on the skin to be removed. Then they are taken from the water and sprinkled with salt and barley flour. After a few weeks the leather is softened by soaking in [treated] water [which] gives the skin its beautiful yellow-brown color.

While Ribbi Haim works he reminds himself of the purpose of his work by repeating 'Le-shem Sefer Torah,' 'destined for the Sefer Torah,' so joining the speech to the thought and the thought to the movement of the hand. He squares off the skin by cutting uneven edges off. Then he scores the skip by tracing with a ruler and a stylus the line which will guide the hand of the sofer. . . . [He] dips his reed, taken from a

array of styles and materials, from wire sculptures, to stained glass, to painted ceramic, to inlaid wood, to colored clay, to filigreed silver. In fact, mezuzah covers are one of the things commonly made by Jewish children in Hebrew school because the main rule is simply that there be a container for the scroll.

The Visual Arts

On the opposite extreme from the charm of a proudly displayed mezuzah made by a child is the dazzling artwork of certain Jewish texts. One art form of the thirteenth through fifteenth centuries is the illuminated manuscript, a book on whose pages intricate and colorful pictures and designs are interwoven with text. The crowning achievement of Jewish illuminated manuscripts is the hundreds of versions of the Passover Haggadah, a book containing the story of the liberation of the Hebrews from slavery

bamboo tree, in a black ink that he prepares with the ashes of gallnut tree wood, gum arabic and copper sulphate. Everyday, seated cross-legged, the skin stretched on his thigh, Ribbi Haim copies the word of G-d saying, 'Le-shem Ketivath Sefer Torah,' 'For the purpose of writing a Sefer Torah.'

When the Torah is finished . . . , the task of authenticating the scroll is just beginning. One of his sons reads aloud and spells the text of the Torah while Ribbi Haim verifies word by word in the scroll, correcting when needed. The sheets of parchment are then sewn together with a

thread made of sheep ligament. The scroll is now ready to be brought like a bride under the Hupah [bridal canopy] to the synagogue to which it is destined."

A decorative encasing protects a Torah scroll.

in Egypt as well as instructions for holding the Seder. Even today, very creative and artistic new versions continue to be printed, including some that look more like comic books than sacred texts, and some specifically geared for young children. Other texts such as the five megillot, or scrolls, are also often illustrated. These include the popular story of Esther, the heroine of Purim, a holiday celebrating her success in foiling a plot against the Jews and saving them from slaughter in Persia; and the story of Ruth, a famous tale of acceptance of the Jewish faith.

The Torah, on the other hand, is not illustrated but it is still a work of art. Torah scrolls, used for reading in the synagogue, are always handwritten in the most exacting of fashions by highly skilled and respected scribes. The document is read by unrolling one continuous scroll from one rod, and taking up the slack onto the other rod. In this way over the course of a year, the whole Torah is read.

Much visual art in synagogues today features Jewish symbols such as the menorah, the Star of David, and the twin tablets of the Ten Commandments. These symbols are very concretely associated with Judaism, but there are more abstract ways to convey Jewish symbolism. Perhaps the best example is the renowned stained glass windows by Marc Chagall, which are housed in the synagogue at the Hadassah Hospital in Ein Kerem, outside Jerusalem. Chagall created twelve windows, representing the twelve tribes, using particular colors, abstract designs, and the occasional recognizable symbol to create a piece reflecting the personality and life story of the founder of each tribe. Many of Chagall's other works, though not specifically for synagogues, also incorporate Jewish symbols. This is characteristic of many painters and other artists of the last century and contemporary times, who introduce Jewish symbolism and stories into their work without creating what might be classified as "religious" art. Of particular renown is the British sculptor Jacob Epstein, who created massive, powerful works some-times inspired by biblical stories. One of his most famous is a depiction of one well-known story in Genesis in which Jacob wrestles all night with a mysterious figure. Epstein's massive work *Jacob and the Angel* is carved in pink marble with simple, larger-than-life, and somewhat abstract human figures intertwined in each other's grip.

Literature and Film

Jewish writers and filmmakers, like visual artists, often incorporate elements of their heritage in their works. Writers admire the Tanakh for its poetic language, compelling stories, and great moral themes, and it became the foundation for the revival of literature written in Hebrew in modern times as well as a major source for writers in other languages. In 1966 novelist Shmuel Yosef Agnon (1888–1970), an Israeli, won the Nobel Prize for literature. Agnon was an Orthodox Jew who learned Hebrew as a second language when he immigrated to Israel. His novels *The Bridal Canopy* and *A Guest for the Night* focus on the struggle to live ethically when religious faith has been shaken.

Internationally acclaimed Amos Oz is probably the best-known Israeli writer of fiction and nonfic-

Israeli writer Amos Oz proudly displays one of his books.

Yehuda Amichai, whose death in 2000 was widely mourned in Israel, and Dan Pagis are two of the best-known poets of recent years.

However, Jewish literature is by no means limited to Israeli writers. In fact, the number of Jewish writers around the world is beyond determining, because this type of intellectual endeavor has always been highly prized by Jews. One measure of this is the ten Nobel Prizes for literature given to Jewish writers, including Henri-Louis Bergson of France, Boris Pasternak and Joseph Brodsky of Russia, Saul Bellow of Canada, Isaac Bashevis Singer of Poland, and Nadine Gordimer of South Africa. Other writers focusing on Jewish themes, such as Philip Roth, Bernard Malamud, Elie Wiesel, and Chaim Potok, are among the best known in the world.

In recent years there has been an explosion of popular fiction featuring life in Jewish communities and families. Some of these focus on the past, such as Anita Diamant's

tion today. Oz, an active member of Peace Now, is a major spokesperson for pacifism in Israel today, and his works focus on the personal and other challenges of living in Israel. Other well-known writers in the last several decades are A.B. Yehoshua, Meir Shalev, Amalia Kahana-Carmon, Ruth Almog, Anton Shammas, and Yossl Birstein, who sets his works in the Orthodox Jewish communities of Israel. Poets are also well represented among writers in Modern Hebrew.

The Red Tent, a retelling of the story of Jacob and his offspring, and Jacob Jaffee's *Land of Dreams,* about American immigrant Jews. Some are multigenerational sagas, such as Tova Mirvis's *The Ladies Auxiliary,* and the numerous works by Maisie Mosco. Younger writers such as Allegra Goodman and Myla Goldberg continue to explore the challenges of Jewish identity and life today.

As with literature, the Jewish contribution to film is incalculable. Israeli films such as Gila Almagor's *The Summer of Aviya* and the sequel *Under the Domin Tree,* about Holocaust survivors, as well as *Shu'ur* by Hannah Azoulai and Shmuel Hasfari and *Coffee with Lemon* by Leonid Govirets, both about the problems of new immigrants, have been critically acclaimed but not widely released outside Israel. However, in the United States since the inception of the film industry, Jews have made their mark in directing, producing, and acting. Woody Allen, Mel Brooks, and Barbra Streisand stand out in particular because they have done all three, and also have made Jewish identity a theme in their work. The film industry received a boost and a nod of recognition in 1967 when a Jewish film archive at Hebrew University in Jerusalem was established, and later named for famed American director and museum benefactor, Stephen Spielberg.

Music

Ability to express oneself musically and to participate in the community through dancing, singing, and playing a musical instrument has always been as central a part of Jewish identity as learning from books. However, outside of the tropes, or set melodies for chanting scripture and prayers, and the exuberant folk music of Jewish communities around the world, until recent years Jewish musicians, songwriters, and composers tended to bypass Jewish themes. For example, there is little in the music of classical composers Felix Mendelssohn and Gustav Mahler to indicate their Jewish backgrounds, and the same is true of more contemporary composers such as Stephen Sondheim. A few composers such as Ernest Bloch, Leonard Bernstein, Darius Milhaud, and Sergey Prokofiev from time to time wrote works using Jewish themes or melodies, primarily those of the cantors in synagogue services. Modern Israeli composers such as Mordechai Seter, however, have incorporated the

Richard Rodgers (left) and Oscar Hammerstein developed an American, rather than Jewish, musical style.

rhythms and melodic styles of Yemeni and other Middle Eastern Jews, eastern Mediterranean musical traditions, and Jewish religious music into what has become known as the Mediterranean style. Paul Ben-Haim, Oedon Partos, and Alexander Uriah Boscoritch have also been pioneers of a distinctly Israeli classical music.

In popular music and other stage performance, a similar pattern of Jewish assimilation emerged. In earlier times, when anti-Semitism was more blatant, assimilation was important except to those artists who cultivated their Jewishness in vaudeville and other stage acts, creating the genre of the Jewish comedian still popular today. In music, however, other than klezmer and other traditional Jewish musical styles, it was best to play down one's roots. Artists such as jazz clarinetist and bandleader Benny Goodman, composers such as Ira and George Gershwin, and Broadway musical creators such as Richard Rodgers and Oscar Hammerstein, strove to create a style that was more generally American than specifically Jewish. Ironically, one Jewish composer

Klezmer Music

The Yiddish-speaking Jews of Eastern Europe had nearly a thousand years in which their Ashkenazic culture developed, and klezmer—a Yiddish word originally based on the Hebrew *klei-zemer,* "vessels of song"—was a large part of that culture. Klezmer began in medieval eastern Europe, where Jewish musicians (klezmorim) traveled between towns for festivals, weddings, and other celebrations in the Jewish community. Klezmorim were an important part of Jewish life in eastern Europe, and their style of music became one of the central means by which immigrants escaping the pogroms maintained continuity with their old-world culture in their new homes in America and elsewhere.

Instrumental music was forbidden in the synagogues of Europe. Yet the melodies and rhythms of chanted prayers and Torah reading, and the ecstatic singing of the Hasidim became part of klezmer music, though for centuries there were no vocals at all. The most popular instruments included violin, clarinet, and accordion. Depending on availability, brass, other reeds, and a double bass might be included. Drums were a rather late addition, as were the vocals often heard today.

By the nineteenth and early twentieth centuries, klezmer music was a well-developed musical style, an example of early fusion music, inspired not just by Jewish religious music, but by other traditional music of the eastern European shtetls and the folk music of local, non-Jewish cultures. The only things absolutely required in klezmer music are an enthusiastic beat, a lively melody, and musicians who love playing. If people are not dancing, it is not klezmer.

of popular music, Irving Berlin, wrote what has become one of the great Christmas classics, "White Christmas," for the film of the same name, as well as music for a movie named for another Christian holiday, *Easter Parade.* Even more modern performers such as Bruce Springsteen and Bob Dylan have dabbled in Jewish themes but have usually looked beyond them to more universal ones.

In fact, the religious background and views of most American musical stars today is an inconsequential part of their music. There are some exceptions, such as Debbie Friedman, a popular Jewish composer and vocalist, Even Sh'siyah, a Jewish rock band from Chicago, and Schlock Rock, a group that takes popular hits and rewrites hilarious lyrics around Jewish themes. In Israel, however, which has one of the world's most exciting popular music scenes, music takes on a more decidedly Jewish flavor. Because most Israeli pop stars sing in Hebrew, many have not achieved the international recognition they might otherwise enjoy. Stars popular in Israel for years include Chava Albertsein, Naomi Shemer, and Airik Einstein. Israel has a number of excellent bands, including Tipex, Gaia, Sheva, and Hachaverim Shel Natasha.

Out of all the arts, some argue that it is in music that the spirit and identity of Jews has been most widely and profoundly expressed.

Indeed the spinning and whirling of David, and the exuberance of his words to the Jews to rejoice in the Lord with song and lyre, would give evidence that this artistic form above all is in the Jewish soul. But the Jewish contribution to all the arts is great beyond description. These contributions reflect the same mix of views about religion and personal identity as felt in the population at large. For some artists, being Jewish is so important it cannot help but be a major theme in their work. For others it is more quietly present while they work on expressing something else. But wherever the individual creative impulse leads, this 2 percent of the world's population has made a dazzling mark.

chapter | seven

Looking Forward, Looking Back

One of Judaism's great strengths is continuity. Though the doctrines and practices of the faith have evolved over the centuries, monotheism and the concept of binding human ethics are built on Abraham's and Moses's framework. However, in every place Jews have lived during the Christian era, that continuity has been threatened in one way or another, sometimes by violence or force from the

A man removes a spray-painted swastika from the gate of a Jewish cemetery. Although Jews have always faced discrimination, the strength of their faith has enabled them to endure.

outside and sometimes by pressures from within. Nevertheless, the overwhelming majority of Jews have never considered conversion to another faith or tried to make their Jewishness invisible. Though countless numbers have lost their lives over the centuries to violent acts of anti-Semitism, and a deluge of laws and other forms of ostracism have often made their situation extraordinarily difficult, the Jewish people have simply refused to become extinct.

Going Beyond Survival

For Jews, the determination to overcome even the most relentless of adversaries is due to more than the simple human desire to survive. Jewish tradition holds that every Jewish soul—past, present, and future —was at Mount Sinai when God gave the commandments. Thus Jewish law is not simply a set of rules passed down through the generations as a matter of tradition. Jews are to act as if they personally gave their word to God that they would observe and do what He commanded. But the symbolism of the collective souls at Mount Sinai is even more profound than that, for it also means that there is one community of Jews that includes all Jews who

have ever lived, all future generations, and all Jews alive today around the globe. To abandon or betray one's identity as a Jew is to disrespect not only the Patriarchs, Judges, Kings, Prophets, and Sages of the biblical past, but also the millions of common people who kept and are keeping the faith and the culture from extinction by simply living day in and day out as Jews. Likewise, the generations yet to come depend on people living today to keep a Jewish culture for them to be born into. In addition to maintaining continuity across the generations, Jews in trouble anywhere in the world are a cause for concern among the others. Even Jews who do not see the relevance of religious faith in their own lives usually feel a sense of loyalty and connectedness at some level to one or more aspects of Jewish culture, history, and community.

Judaism remains, therefore, for most Jews, at some deep level, synonymous with a far-flung, intergenerational family. In the typical family, members' personalities vary widely, the different generations and branches of the family tree are not always viewed with equal respect, disagreements are often intense and even hostile, and individual variations from family norms

The Death of Daniel Pearl

Daniel Pearl, an American Jew, was a reporter for the prestigious *Wall Street Journal,* and by all accounts was a dedicated journalist. He was only thirty-eight years old in January 2002 when he was kidnapped, tortured, and killed in Karachi, Pakistan, while researching a story on the Islamic militant underground. Grisly videos detailed his torture and violent death at the hands of terrorists. Initially his abductors claimed he was an agent for the CIA, but later they changed their story, claiming he was actually an agent for Mossad, the Israeli intelligence agency. The truth was he was simply a reporter, willing to go with them to get the story despite the risks.

Pearl was the child of Israeli immigrants to the United States. He was proud to be Jewish, but was not, according to those who knew him, religiously observant. In the seconds before his throat was slit, Pearl's captors had him say, "My father is a Jew, my mother is a Jew, and I am a Jew." Those were his last words. Though the American and other media played down this aspect of Pearl's death, for the Jewish community it was a clear signal that blind hatred is still a potentially deadly threat in many places in the world, and that this is not clearly enough understood by non-Jews.

are often a source of conflict. So it is with the worldwide family of Jews. Their diversity in and of itself creates dissension, and the passion with which many Jews treat fundamental issues such as what being Jewish entails or how Judaism can maintain its integrity in a changing world is testament to how important the survival of Judaism is to most Jews. The nearly endless variety of views on all subjects impacting Jews makes the task of summarizing what it means to be a Jew today a very difficult

proposition. Some concerns, however, are held in common regardless of where and how the world's Jews live.

Conflicts Within the Faith

Perhaps the biggest challenge to Judaism today is the deep division within the faith between Orthodoxy and the rest of Judaism. Though it would be inaccurate to say that all Orthodox Jews feel one particular way, there is a strong sentiment within Orthodoxy, particularly among the most rigidly observant, that there is only one way to practice Judaism. That way is to organize and live one's life around the commandments of the Torah. Those who do not scrupulously adhere to the mitzvot are by parentage still Jews, but they are not regarded by the Orthodox as adherents to Judaism. In other words, in the eyes of many Orthodox, any Jew who eats shrimp, or smokes on the Sabbath, or does not recite the Shema evening and morning has abandoned the covenant and cannot claim to be a faithful, practicing Jew.

This rigorous definition of Judaism has created a great deal of tension. In the United States, both Reform and Conservative Jews take issue with the view that only the Orthodox are truly maintaining the faith. For the most part, the fact that the groups worship in different places keeps conflict between them to a minimum, but from time to time problems arise. For example, an Orthodox rabbi would refuse to officiate at a wedding if the bride or groom had been converted to Judaism by a Reform rabbi, because he would not accept the conversion as valid, and he would not officiate at any wedding except between two Jews. A Jew who strictly observes the laws of kashruth will not eat anything served on plates from a nonkosher kitchen, even if the food itself follows the dietary laws. Some Jewish hosts will good-naturedly pull out the paper plates and plastic utensils, but many are insulted by the implication that they are not proper Jews.

In Israel the conflict between Orthodox and other Jews takes a different form. The distinction there is really only between "religious," or observant, and "nonreligious," or secular, Jews. Approximately three-quarters of Israelis categorize themselves as the latter. The hostile views widely held by one group toward the other create an extremely negative dynamic in the country. The problem is aggravated by the very public positions taken by extremely conservative Orthodox groups such as the Haredim. Whereas in the United States, Orthodoxy has little impact on nonobservant Jews, every secular Israeli Jew is subject to restrictive policies reflecting Orthodox views. In recent years the most extreme elements of Orthodox Judaism have become very powerful politically in the *Knesset*, the Israeli congress, and in combination with religious leaders they have made life difficult for nonobservant Jews. All Jewish weddings

The Knesset *meets in Jerusalem. Orthodox* Knesset *members have been able to pass many conservative religious laws in Israel.*

in Israel must be performed by an Orthodox rabbi, and if a question about the Jewish heritage or the religiosity of a bride or groom comes up, the couple simply cannot be married in Israel unless the problem can be resolved to the rabbi's satisfaction. Similar constraints are put on Jewish burials. Non-Orthodox converts from the United States and elsewhere are not treated as Jews at all when they immigrate, despite the rigor of their personal religious practices, and many find the obstacles to Orthodox conver-

sion are so great in Israel that they can never become halakically, or legally, Jewish. A recent proposal in the *Knesset* to lump congregations other than Orthodox into the same "non-Jewish" category as Christians and Muslims for purposes of determining government subsidies shows the extent to which the followers of extreme forms of Orthodoxy are unprepared to acknowledge differences in viewpoint among Jews.

The social problem in Israel is aggravated by the fact that many of the most rigidly Orthodox are excused from otherwise obligatory military service, and many do not hold paying jobs. Instead, they choose a life of studying Torah. Their living expenses are paid by their study center, or yeshiva, but Israeli taxpayers support the yeshiva. Thus secular Israeli taxpayers endure criticisms of their lack of commitment to Judaism from the same people whose own commitment to Judaism they are supporting with their taxes—a major source of resentment in Israel today. Adding to the resentment is the fact that due to Orthodox political clout, Israel gives welfare bonuses for having large families. Orthodox families tend to be large, and every additional child is thus supported financially either partly or wholly by secular Israelis. Many young secular Israelis must think twice about how they will be able to afford starting their own families at all, in part because taxes are astronomically high, and they often are critical of what they perceive as unequal treatment. Many secular Jews, however, recognize that their lifestyles are not helping to sustain Judaism and that their history is a caution against becoming too complacent. Therefore many who complain about supporting a group who does not support them in re-

turn do at least credit religiously observant Israelis with keeping Judaism alive.

Anti-Semitism

Though the Orthodox have very restrictive ideas about who is and is not a Jew, the most commonly accepted view is that anyone with a Jewish mother is a Jew. Reform Jews accept as a Jew anyone who has one Jewish parent and was raised in a Jewish home. However, these definitions have meant little outside the Jewish community. Wherever Jews have been discriminated against or physically harmed for their faith, their attackers have cared little about the details of their victims' lineage. The Nazis, for example, treated anyone as Jewish who had one Jewish grandparent, with the idea of eradicating altogether the supposed Jewish "race." Before legal challenges ended discriminatory practices in the United States, employment, educational, and other opportunities such as the chance to live in particular neighborhoods were frequently denied based on a person's last name alone. Applicants to universities were often required to submit photos, the idea being that the admission committee would be able to tell a Jew just by looking.

A Nazi soldier executes a Jewish man. Although anti-Semitism was more flagrant in Nazi Europe, it still exists in many forms.

raelis escalated in 1999. In many places around the world individual Jews, usually traditionally dressed Orthodox men, are sometimes verbally and physically attacked in the streets. In the United States, Jewish cemeteries and synagogues are desecrated even today. Such occurrences are distressing reminders of how the fervor against Jews was fanned in Nazi-era Europe, and there is a deep-seated fear among Jews that bad times may lie ahead. The announced intention of radical Muslims to target Jews lends urgency to those concerns. Many Jews believe that, despite the official apologies of some nations and Christian religions for their part in or indifference during the Holocaust, nothing really has changed.

Anti-Semitism is still very widespread in the world today. Radical Muslims, focused on the destruction of Israel and the Jews, have found fertile ground in Europe and elsewhere. In France a number of synagogues and Jewish social centers have been firebombed or otherwise vandalized since tensions between Palestinians and Is-

Defending Israel

Part of the reason for the pessimism of many Jews is the complicated situation posed by the continuing violence between Jews and Palestinians in Israel. Some Jews, particularly extremely Orthodox ones, are opposed to the existence of a Jewish state at all, claiming that a sovereign land for the Jews is only supposed to occur when the Messianic Age comes, and thus today's Israel is in direct opposition to God's will rather than a fulfillment of it. Some Jews, both in Israel and elsewhere, feel strongly that Israel has violated Jewish ethical heritage with its political and military policies toward the Palestinians, and though they support the existence of a homeland they are very upset with how that homeland has been evolving. But the typical Israeli Jew and the majority of Jews elsewhere in the world are extremely supportive of Israel even though they may not approve of everything it does.

The fervor with which American and other Jews view Israel as a

Peace Now

The largest of Israel's peace activist groups is Peace Now, founded in 1978 by several hundred reserve officers and soldiers of the Israel Defense Forces. Its goal is to pressure the Israeli government to negotiate mutual compromises with neighboring Arab countries and Palestinians to bring peace and security to Israel. It advocates, for example, that Israel withdraw from the Golan Heights, a border region with Syria, in the hope of achieving peace with that nation. It also calls for recognizing the rights of the Palestinians to their own independent state.

Peace Now is opposed to settlements in the West Bank and Gaza Strip, where a future independent Palestinian state is proposed. Its main activities include protest rallies, lobbying activities, and court challenges to any further growth in Israeli settlements in those areas. It also protests use of tax money on settlements that could be better used on social services in Israel or simply not collected from financially burdened Israelis in the first place. Peace Now also monitors the situation of Palestinian residents of East Jerusalem, who are frequently subject to restrictions on movement and on construction projects, which the organization views as violations of equal rights. One of the major focuses of Peace Now is joint activities such as vigils and marches, and discussion groups involving mixed groups of Israeli and Palestinian youth. The youth wing also sponsors bicycle trips, marathons, and other projects designed to promote peace. Worldwide branches of Peace Now have also been established, including in the United States.

symbol of Jewish survival is reflected in their support of many causes, including ones as diverse as buying ambulances for Magen David Adom, the "Israeli Red Cross," and sponsoring free trips to Israel for Jewish American teenagers who wish to learn about their heritage. Supporters of Israel have also lobbied tirelessly to ensure that the United States does not waver in its support for Israel. Israel is a tiny country bordered by Jordan and Egypt, with which it has only uneasy agreements to coexist, and Syria and Lebanon, which remain more active adversaries. Israel is the only non-Muslim country in the Middle East, and the tensions and violence over the issue of a Palestinian state have made Israel's ultimate survival a matter of great concern not only within the country but also around the world.

Most Jews, including Israelis, understand the importance of hav-

Armed Palestinians take up shooting positions in Ramallah in the West Bank. Even today, Israel is a nation with an uncertain future.

ing a homeland and believe the Palestinians should have their own state. However they question where that homeland might be located and what kind of government it might have. Looking at a map of the region, it is easy to appreciate the Israelis' fear that they will be overrun by a hostile Arab world if a new sovereign nation with a history of animosity toward them were to be established along an indefensible border across the hills and deserts of the region. Suicide bombers and other terrorists today can easily slip from the towns and camps of the West Bank into other parts of Israel. If a Palestinian state were declared in the West Bank, as is proposed, Israel would be less than ten miles wide at some points. Thus, a hostile government would be located only minutes away from Tel Aviv, Haifa, and Jerusalem, the three largest cities, which with their suburbs are home to the vast majority of Israelis. A sovereign nation of Palestine would be free to form an army, purchase weapons, make alliances with Iraq and other sworn enemies of Israel, and demand that Israel stay out of its territory even if known terrorists were harbored there. It would be very dangerous for Israel to support the creation of a sovereign na-

tion of Palestine until Palestine shows convincingly that it is prepared to be a peaceful neighbor.

The problem, as many see it, is that radical Muslim groups such as Hamas do not want a peaceful solution because their openly professed goal is to destroy Israel and turn over present Israeli lands to the Palestinians. Thus, it is unlikely at this point that the security of the Jewish state could be achieved by an agreement between the Israeli and Palestinian governments alone. Added to the problem is that many Jews feel that the entire region is their promised land, and they oppose any turnover of land to the Palestinians, particularly because some of the holiest Jewish sites such as Hebron, where the Patriarchs are said to be buried, are located in the West Bank. Some holding these viewpoints deliberately settle in the West Bank as a way of making that point, and in Hebron and elsewhere deadly conflicts frequently erupt.

Declining Numbers

The deaths of Jews at the hands of Palestinians make headlines, but a more subtle force is producing overall declines in the Jewish population of Israel. Except among

"A Scorched Spiritual Soil": Haredi Rabbis Speak

Fewer than 5 percent of the Jews in Israel are Haredim, the most extreme of Orthodox Jews. Their very strict interpretation of the Torah has often put them at odds with other Israeli Jews. Nevertheless they wield tremendous political clout in Israel today, and their openly hostile views have created political and social strife. *HEMDAT,* an online council and clearinghouse for issues relating to religious freedom in Israel, quotes one member of the Chief Rabbinate Council in Jerusalem as saying publicly that "Reform Jews are worse than Christians and war should be declared against them." The prominent editor of an ultra-Orthodox newspaper wrote that "Reform Rabbis are further from Judaism than Christians and Moslems and . . . they should be judged as filthy, lying, vermin who are criminals, [and] who brought about the holocaust on the Jewish people." The leader of the ultra-Orthodox Shas party recently declared that "Reform Jews should be vomited up . . . and thrown out of the country."

When asked to participate in discussions of Jewish identity in Israel, according to another online resource, *Hofesh,* the rabbinic response was to say,

"There is one Jewish identity! Judaism is Judaism and it is not open for discussion. . . . What we can do is to put the Torah, as one whole, in front of their eyes. If they wish, they can avail themselves. If they don't wish, we have nothing to give them in return. The flowerbeds of the Israeli people have almost become plowed over, a scorched spiritual soil."

The attitudes of the Haredim sometimes spill over into vandalism against non-Orthodox synagogues, physical assaults against people perceived as violating the Torah through immodest dress or smoking on Shabbat, and extremely strict control of children. Today, an Internet search using the keyword "Haredi" will pull up a number of sites connected to helping young people escape what to some seems like an extremist cult, but to others is a divinely sanctioned way of life.

the Orthodox, Jewish families tend to be small. Parents often pour whatever resources and time they have into an only child, or perhaps two children at most, and as a result the population of Israel is gradually becoming less Jewish. Today approximately 80 percent of Israelis are Jews, but Arab Israelis, who often have large families, are growing noticeably as a percentage of the population. Jews are concerned that as a democracy, Israel will lose its Jewish character as its population shifts, and that the only Jewish nation in the world will disappear not by being driven into the sea, but by its own dwindling numbers.

Though this situation is far from being a crisis at this time, it is reflected around the world as well. Jews constitute only 2 percent of the world's population, and if their numbers dwindle in certain places such as France and the United States, where many Muslims also live, Jews are concerned that their political power will gradually be eroded in favor of the group most hostile to them. Indeed, many acts of vandalism and street violence against Jews in France and elsewhere have been attributed to Muslims or

Three Grand Rabbis visit graves in Paris that have been vandalized by an organization called the New French Nazi Front.

sympathizers with radical Muslim groups. Though bad behavior by individuals can never be entirely stopped, the Jews' concern is that criminal acts against them and their property seem to result in superficial denouncements by government leaders, but no real plan of action to protect them as citizens. This is reminiscent of how their civil rights eroded over time into the nightmare of the Holocaust. As a result, Jews today are extremely sensitive to what they perceive as, if not outright anti-Semitism, the indifference of the world to their well-being.

Two other factors contribute to a declining Jewish population. The first is a loss of Jewish identity through intermarriage. When a Jew marries a person of Christian heritage, their children may be lost to the Jewish community because they are often raised in neither faith or as Christians. Most rabbis of all denominations refuse to preside at intermarriages, a stance that has created alienation among many Jews who wish to be married as their ancestors had been, but to choose to marry whomever they wish.

The second factor is a general decline over the last generations in religious observance even among unquestionably Jewish families.

Many simply do not attend or join temples or synagogues, observe most Jewish holidays, or have their children go through bar mitzvah or bat mitzvah training because they feel their Jewish identity is not tied to these things. Yet most still do identify to some extent with being Jewish. They circumcise their sons as the mark of the covenant, and they may use Yiddish slang and eat Jewish foods with a special sense of ownership. They may even follow traditions such as putting a mezuzah on the door of their home, simply because they have always had one. In short, they feel little religious commitment nor any need to either disguise or announce their heritage.

Women and Judaism

If asked what the heart of that Jewish heritage is, many would argue that it is the Jewish woman. Judaism is in many respects a very patriarchal faith, but this sense of male domination has largely been limited to the public sphere. In the home it is generally the woman who sets the tone, and the home, for many Jews, is where the faith and the culture are most clearly learned and embraced. Women have what is considered the privilege of preparing the house for Shabbat, one of the most holy and spiritually rewarding aspects of life. In observant homes it is she who makes sure that kosher rules are kept, a practice that is seen as creating a sense of personal connectedness to the divine. Though couples share the duties of a Jewish education for their children, it is the mother who is revered for bringing them into the world. A Jewish marriage is meant to be an equal partnership in all respects, and living as a Jewish family entails important roles for both husband and wife.

However, in the larger community there are many traditions that convey a sense of second-class status to women. Until non-Orthodox denominations inaugurated changes in recent years, only men could be rabbis or cantors. Orthodox syna-gogues today still have separate seating areas for men and women, and women do not come forward to participate as readers or pronouncers of blessings. Women are not counted in the ten people required for a minyan. They do not put on tefillin or prayer shawls (although recently they have begun putting on the tallith, if they wish, in some non-Orthodox congregations). The bat mitzvah, the coming of age ceremony for girls, did not exist until Mordecai Kaplan, the founder of Reconstructionist Judaism, adapted the bar mitzvah ceremony for his daughter.

In defense of these practices, traditionalist Jews argue that the reasons behind them are that women have a special status that is

A Jewish girl reads from the Torah during her bat mitzvah Historically, Jewish women have been accorded a second-class status.

in no way secondary. They are excused from ritual obligations in the synagogue because they are presumed to be too busy to participate. They are not counted in a minyan so as to relieve any sense of pressure to go to the synagogue to ensure there is a minyan. They do not put on tefillin or prayer shawls because they are not obligated to observe the rituals that require them. They must sit in a separate section of the synagogue because of the distraction from prayer that the presence of both sexes in proximity can cause. Though many find these explanations satisfactory, others point out that if the location of the women's section is hidden away on a balcony or otherwise out of view of the service, this is hardly a statement of spiritual equality and forbidding a woman to participate in religious observances is far different from simply excusing her. Furthermore, Jewish feminists point out, "women's work," meaning duties in the home, is not valued in modern culture to the same extent as "men's work" outside. Thus, people can claim that differences in treatment are a way of honoring the Jewish women, but it does not

really feel that way to many of them.

Despite the many fractures within Judaism today, it remains true that most Jews relate to each other as members of a community, however fragile and variously defined that community might be. Judaism's greatest strength perhaps is that Jews continue to feel that being Jewish is important, regardless of how they make it, or do not make it, part of their daily lives and immediate sense of identity. When Jews meet, they know there is an element of commonality of experience that comes from being a minority with a very special shared history and culture. Most of the people in the typical Jew's world are not Jewish and thus do not know Jewish prayers, religious or ethnic vocabulary, or traditions, and therefore meeting another Jew implies an unspoken kind of sharing that is meaningful. Traditionalists would say that sense of sharing runs all the way back to the thunder they all heard when God appeared before them at Mount Sinai and created the covenant that has bound them to each other, and to Him, ever since.

Notes

Introduction: One God, One People, Many Voices

1. Stephen M. Wylen, *Settings of Silver: An Introduction to Judaism.* New York: Paulist Press, 1989, p. 3.
2. *Tanakh: The Holy Scriptures.* Philadelphia: Jewish Publication Society, 1985, p. 1115.

Chapter 1: Patriarchs and Promises

3. Chaim Potok, *Wanderings: Chaim Potok's History of the Jews.* New York: Fawcett Crest Books, 1978, p. 32.
4. *Tanakh: The Holy Scriptures,* p. 89.
5. Leo Trepp, *A History of the Jewish Experience.* Springfield, N.J.: Behrman House, 2001, p. 20.
6. *Tanakh: The Holy Scriptures,* p. 225.
7. *Tanakh: The Holy Scriptures,* p. 241.
8. *Tanakh: The Holy Scriptures,* p. 291.
9. *Tanakh: The Holy Scriptures,* p. 291.

Chapter 2: Life in the Promised Land

10. Raymond P. Scheindlin, *A Short History of the Jewish People.* Oxford: Oxford University Press, 1998, p. 7.
11. Potok, *Wanderings,* p. 123.
12. Potok, *Wanderings,* p. 123.
13. Scheindlin, *A Short History of the Jewish People,* p. 22.
14. *Tanakh: The Holy Scriptures,* p. 1272.
15. Scheindlin, *A Short History of the Jewish People,* p. 23.
16. Scheindlin, *A Short History of the Jewish People,* p. 33.
17. Scheindlin, *A Short History of the Jewish People,* p. 43.
18. Trepp, *A History of the Jewish Experience,* p. 81.

Chapter 3: Jews and Their Communities

19. Wylen, *Settings of Silver,* p. 174.
20. *Tanakh: The Holy Scriptures,* p. 989.
21. Scheindlin, *A Short History of the Jewish People,* p. 85.
22. Scheindlin, *A Short History of the Jewish People,* p. 151.
23. Louis Jacobs, *The Oxford Concise Companion to the Jewish Religion.* Oxford: Oxford University Press, 1999, p. 94.
24. Trepp, *A History of the Jewish Experience,* p. 173.
25. Scheindlin, *A Short History of the Jewish People,* p. 160.
26. Scheindlin, *A Short History of the Jewish People,* p. 166.

Chapter 4: Jewish Philosophy and Beliefs

27. Quoted in George Robinson, *Essential Judaism: A Complete Guide to Beliefs, Customs, and Rituals.* New York: Pocket Books, 2000, p. 235.
28. Wylen, *Settings of Silver,* p. 175.
29. Adin Steinsaltz, *The Essential Talmud.* N.p.: Basic Books, 1976, p. 56.
30. Quoted in Wayne Dosick, *Living Judaism.* San Francisco: HarperSanFrancisco, 1990, p. 64.
31. Trepp, *A History of the Jewish Experience,* p. 143.

32. Dosick, *Living Judaism*, p. 61.
33. Dosick, *Living Judaism*, p. 62.
34. Quoted in Trepp, *A History of the Jewish Experience*, p. 177.
35. Robinson, *Essential Judaism*, p. 193.

Chapter 5: Living a Jewish Life

36. Robinson, *Essential Judaism*, p. 20.
37. Dosick, *Living Judaism*, p. 205.
38. Robinson, *Essential Judaism*, p.33.
39. C.M. Pilkington, *Teach Yourself Judaism*. Chicago: NTC Publishing Group, 2000, p. 89.
40. Pilkington, *Teach Yourself Judaism*, p. 90.
41. Quoted in Stephen J. Einstein and Lydia Kukoff, *Every Person's Guide to Judaism*. New York: UAHC Press, 1989, p. 100.
42. Trepp, *A History of the Jewish Experience*, p. 408.
43. Dosick, *Living Judaism*, p. 133.
44. Trepp, *A History of the Jewish Experience*, p. 406.
45. Dosick, *Living Judaism*, p. 137.

Chapter 6: New Songs and Ancient Themes: Jewish Arts and Culture

46. *Tanakh: The Holy Scriptures*, p. 479.
47. *Tanakh: The Holy Scriptures*, p. 1142.
48. Dosick, *Living Judaism*, p. 225.

Glossary

Aggadah: Jewish traditional literature on nonlegal subjects (see halakah). Aggadah treats Jewish history, folklore, medicine, astronomy, popular stories, proverbs, among other subjects.

ark of the covenant: The container, or chest, built to hold the stone tablets of the Ten Commandments. Today, the cabinet or other container used in synagogues to hold the Torah scrolls is also called an ark.

Bible: General term used by Christians to refer to the "Old" and "New" Testaments, and by Jews to refer only to the "Old" Testament.

covenant: A pact of mutual obligation, especially between God and the children of Israel, today's Jews.

diaspora: Dispersal of a people exiled from their homeland.

get: A document given by a husband to a wife that ends their marriage in accordance with Jewish law.

Haggadah: "The telling." Generally used in reference to the special book used to celebrate the Passover Seder.

halakah: Jewish law, as laid down in the Torah and expounded upon by later Jewish scholars in the Talmud and other sources.

Holocaust: Referred to in Hebrew as ha-Shoah, the term used to cover all the events of the Nazi Era directed toward the extermination of the Jews.

mezuzah: From the Hebrew word for "doorpost." A case enclosing a small scroll containing words from the Shema directing Jews to affix a reminder of God's eminence in their lives to their doorposts and gates.

midrash: From the Hebrew words for inquiry or investigation. The means by which the ancient rabbis searched the Torah for hidden meanings, interpreted its laws, and created explanations of events or concepts.

minyan: A group of ten adult Jews, the minimum necessary for communal prayer. In Orthodoxy, all members of a minyan must be male.

Mishnah: The earliest digest of the written and Oral Torah, undertaken by Judah ha-Nasi.

mitzvah/mitzvot (pl.): From the Hebrew word for "command." Used to delineate the 613 laws given to Moses at Mount Sinai. The term is also used loosely to mean "good deed."

Oral Torah: Used to refer to those aspects of Jewish law and custom that are not specifically laid down in the Torah but are considered binding on Jews, either because they were given privately to Moses by God or deduced from the written Torah by the Sages and other scholars.

Orthodox Judaism: Modern-era term used to denote Jews who strictly follow Jewish law (halakah) and traditional Jewish customs, as codified in the Shulkhan Arukh. Many Orthodox Jews prefer the term "Torah-true."

Pale of Settlement: An area along the western edge of the Russian Empire, including today's Poland and Ukraine, where Jews were forced to live in the nineteenth and early twentieth centuries.

Reform Judaism: Nineteenth-century German movement arguing that Judaism should be reinterpreted so that Jews could more easily practice the faith within the context of modern life and thought.

Sabbath: General term used by Christians and Jews for the seventh day, on which God is said to have rested from the work of creation. The Jewish term is Shabbat or Shabbos. It is observed from sundown Friday to nightfall Saturday, determined by the point at which three stars can be seen in the darkening sky.

secular: A term used to denote anything nonreligious or nonsacred. Also used to describe a person who does not observe the practices of his or her faith.

Seder: From the Hebrew word for "order." The term used for the special celebration and dinner on the first, and in some cases also the second, night of Passover.

synagogue: A building in which Jews congregate to offer prayers, and which often serves as a center for promoting Jewish identity in communities where they are a small minority. Usually called a temple by Reform Jews. Also called "shul," from the Yiddish word for school, denoting the synagogue's larger role as a place of learning.

Talmud: A work containing the teaching of Jewish scholars of the first few centuries A.D., designed as a running commentary to the Mishnah.

Tanakh: The term often used by Jews to denote the Hebrew Bible, so as to avoid confusion with the Christian Bible, which includes the "New" Testament. The term is an acronym for its three parts: Torah, Nevi'im (Prophets), and Ketuvim (the Writings).

Temple/temple: Capitalized, a reference to the building in Jerusalem that served as the center of worship for early Jews. Lowercase, one of the terms used for a modern center of Jewish worship.

Torah: The first five books of the Tanakh, including Exodus, in which Moses receives the 613 mitzvot that define the covenant of the children of Israel with God.

yeshiva: An educational institution focusing exclusively on the scholarly study of the Torah and other important Jewish texts.

For Further Reading

Miriam Chaikin, *Angels Sweep the Desert Floor: Bible Legends about Moses in the Wilderness.* N.p.: Clarion Books, 2002. Midrash stories about Moses in a well-illustrated volume.

————, *Menorahs, Mezuzas, and Other Jewish Symbols.* N.p.: Clarion Books, 1990. Well-illustrated explanation of the significance of important Jewish objects.

Hasia R. Diner, *A New Promised Land: A History of Jews in America.* Oxford: Oxford University Press, 2002. Excellent work covering immigration, current lifestyles, and contributions of Jews to American history and culture.

Levi S. Jacob and Ralphy E. Jhirad, *Judaism.* Leicester, England: Silverdale Books, 2000. Well-illustrated and clearly written basic text on Judaism.

Sondra Leiman and Jonathan D. Sarna, *America: The Jewish Experience.* New York: UAHC Press, 1994. Well-researched book containing color photos, maps, and literature explaining the experience of American immigrants in a very readable style.

Kenny Mann, *The Ancient Hebrews.* Tarrytown, NY: Marshall Cavendish, 1999. Good, clear discussion of the Jews' early history.

Gedalia Peterseil, *Tell It From the Torah.* New York: Pitspopany Press, 1998. A book designed to help young readers understand the meaning of Torah stories.

Eric Ray, *Sofer: The Story of a Torah Scroll.* Los Angeles, CA: Tora, Aura, 1998. Short but interesting book by a Torah scribe describing the process of making a Torah scroll.

Deborah Spector Siegal, *The Cross by Day, the Mezuzah by Night.* Philadelphia: JPS, 1999. Compelling young adult fiction about a Jewish girl who tries to save her family and faith during the Inquisition in Spain.

Milton Steinberg, *As a Driven Leaf.* Springfield, NJ: Behrman House, 1939. Very readable and interesting novel about Palestine during the Roman occupation.

Daniel B. Syme, *The Jewish Home: A Guide for Jewish Living.* New York: UAHC Press, 1988. Good discussion of essential elements of Jewish life arranged in a question and answer format.

Stephen M. Wylen, *The Book of the Jewish Year.* New York: UAHC Press, 1996. Excellent, well-illustrated volume with many interesting sidebars about Jewish celebrations and their backgrounds.

Works Consulted

Books

Nicholas De Lange, *An Introduction to Judaism.* Cambridge: Cambridge University Press, 2000. Good overview of Judaism with strong sections on Jews and their place in the world today.

Hayim Halevy Donin, *To Be a Jew.* N.p.: Basic Books, 1972. A very thorough discussion of Jewish rituals and regulations.

————, *To Pray as a Jew.* N.p.: Basic Books, 1980. A classic volume presenting each service and other prayer rituals in great detail, along with explanations of their point and importance.

Wayne Dosick, *Living Judaism.* San Francisco: HarperSanFrancisco, 1995. Extremely well-written and thoughtful discussion of the entire range of subjects essential to an understanding of Judaism, with a number of essays on intriguing subjects such as Jewish views of right and wrong and how to pray.

Stephen J. Einstein and Lydia Kukoff, *Every Person's Guide to Judaism.* New York: UAHC Press, 1989. Easily understood and well-illustrated general discussion.

Louis Jacobs, *The Oxford Concise Companion to the Jewish Religion.* Oxford: Oxford University Press, 1999. Encyclopedia-style volume, good for quick reference, but many entries are not very clear.

C.M. Pilkington, *Teach Yourself Judaism.* Chicago: NTC Publishing Group, 2000. Clearly written volume with good information about all aspects of the faith.

Chaim Potok, *Wanderings: Chaim Potok's History of the Jews.* New York: Fawcett Crest Books, 1978. Acclaimed imaginative history of the Jewish people organized around themes such as Judaism's relationship with Christianity and Islam.

Dennis Prager and Joseph Telushkin, *Why the Jews? The Reason for Anti-Semitism.* New York: Touchstone Books, 1983. Very well-written and easy-to-understand discussion of the roots of anti-Semitism.

George Robinson, *Essential Judaism: A Complete Guide to Beliefs, Customs, and Rituals.* New York: Pocket Books, 2000. Outstanding one-volume work containing a wealth of information in thorough, readable entries.

Raymond P. Scheindlin, *A Short History of the Jewish People.* Oxford: Oxford University Press, 1998. Good, if sometimes dry, overview of Jewish history from Abraham until contemporary times, with outstanding sidebars focusing in more depth on related subjects of interest.

Huston Smith, *The World's Religions.* San Francisco: HarperSanFrancisco, 1991. Good, if somewhat abstract chapter on Judaism.

Milton Steinberg, *Basic Judaism*. N.p.: Harvest Books, 1986. One of the true classics on the subject.

Adin Steinsaltz, *The Essential Talmud*. N.p.: Basic Books, 1976. Very readable discussion of a difficult subject.

Tanakh: The Holy Scriptures. Philadelphia: The Jewish Publication Society, 1985. Acclaimed modern translation of the Hebrew Bible.

Leo Trepp, *A History of the Jewish Experience*. Springfield, N.J.: Behrman House, 2001. Very well-written and illustrated volume, stressing history and other subjects as they affect the way Jews view themselves.

Stephen M. Wylen, *Settings of Silver: An Introduction to Judaism*. New York: Paulist Press, 1989. Outstanding summary of the teachings and cultural aspects of Judaism.

Internet Source

Shmuel Miller, "Inspiration and Craft: Becoming a Scribe," *TorahSofer*, 2000. www.torahsofer.com.

Websites

HEMDAT (www.hemdat.org). Website sponsored by the Council for Freedom of Science, Religion and Culture, focusing among other things on issues relating to Israeli Orthodoxy.

Hofesh (www.hofesh.org.il). Israeli website focusing on the conflict between Orthodox and secular Jews in Israel.

Index

Picture Credits

About the Author

Laurel Corona lives in Lake Arrowhead, California, and teaches English and humanities at San Diego City College. She has a master's degree from the University of Chicago and a Ph.D. from the University of California at Davis. Dr. Corona has written many other books for Lucent Books, including *Life in Moscow*, *Poland*, *France*, *Israel*, and *The World Trade Center*.